(Continued)

LANGUAGE
CROSSINGS

Negotiating the Self
in a
Multicultural World

KAREN L. OGULNICK
Editor

Teachers College, Columbia University
New York and London

Published by Teachers College Press, 1234 Amsterdam Avenue, New York, NY 10027

Library of Congress Cataloging-in-Publication Data

Language crossings : negotiating the self in a multicultural world / Karen L. Ogulnick, editor.
    p. cm. — (Language and literacy series)
    Includes bibliographical references and index.
    ISBN 0-8077-3999-5 (cloth)—ISBN 0-8077-3998-7 (pbk.)
      1. Second language acquisition. 2. Language and culture. 3. Intercultural communication. I. Ogulnick, Karen, 1960– II. Language and literacy series (New York, N.Y.)
    P118.2 .L364 2000
    418—dc21   00-044337

ISBN 0-8077-3998-7 (paper)
ISBN 0-8077-3999-5 (cloth)

Printed on acid-free paper
Manufactured in the United States of America

08 07 06 05 04 03   8 7 6 5 4 3 2

This book is dedicated to the memory
of my grandparents,
Louis and Mary Ogulnick,
who first taught me what it means
to be an immigrant.

Contents

Part II
MOTHER TONGUES

Part III
THE DIFFICULTIES OF LANGUAGE LEARNING

Part IV
OUR LOVE AFFAIRS WITH LANGUAGES:
STORIES OF MULTI-LANGUAGE LEARNERS

Part V
CLOSE ENCOUNTERS WITH OTHER CULTURES:
LEARNING LANGUAGE WHILE LIVING ABROAD

Acknowledgments

Deep appreciation goes to all the contributors who have written these wondrous self-portraits. I thank everyone for sharing so much of themselves, and for their patience—not to mention the many e-mails, long-distance phone calls, and express mail packages.

I thank Robert Roth for all of his thoughtful conversations, careful readings, and help with recruiting contributors. I also thank the following individuals for their key advice and helpful suggestions at critical stages of this work: Stephanie Hart, Hal Sirowitz, Arnold Sacher, Susan Stocker, Raimundo Mora, Steve Cannon, George Jochnowitz, Greta Hofmann Nemeroff, and Carolina Mancuso.

A special thank you to Berenice Fisher for her suggestion that I put this book together during a stimulating discussion we had at my doctoral defense.

I am grateful to John Mayher and Franklin Horowitz for their positive reviews of this manuscript in its early stages.

Thank you to Carol Chambers Collins for her enthusiasm and faith in this project and for all her work shepherding this book through Teachers College Press, and to Catherine Bernard for her help with editing.

At Long Island University/C.W. Post College I'd like to express my appreciation to the Research Committee for awarding me release time to work on this book, the School of Education for providing me with the support of a graduate assistant, and to Ina Hsien Chiu, who helped enormously with the computer work she did for me.

I thank Megumi Yaginuma for her wonderful photography on the cover.

I'd also like to thank my family for their emotional support, and finally, to anyone I may have forgotten to mention, thank you, too.

Introduction

When I started this project I thought people would write interesting stories about their experiences learning languages. What has transpired amazed me. In talking about something as immense and all-consuming as language, life stories have been told. The meditative, reflective nature of the narratives brought to surface memories of spiritual awakenings; love affairs; political struggles; and conflicts in families, classrooms, and communities. What people chose to spotlight, as well as what they concealed altogether, I'm sure has been illuminating to them as well. As Robert Frost said about writing poetry, "No surprise for the writer, no surprise for the reader" (quoted in Murray, 1990, p. 101).

Something else that surprised me was the eagerness and enthusiasm with which people told their language-learning stories. Even though many of the pieces are associated with pain and struggle, the authors embraced the opportunity to reflect on experiences that have had enormous impacts on their lives. Many writers describe language learning or even just attempting to learn another language as an act of transformation. The opportunity to transcend the self, to travel, and to be another person draws some people into other linguistic worlds; others describe the experience in terms of a loss of a prior self, which has been changed in significant ways after undergoing a process of second-language dominance and cultural assimilation.

I first began to understand the dialectic between language and identity while learning Japanese. Writing about my experiences as a language learner (Ogulnick, 1998) helped to confirm the vague sensation that I was developing a new consciousness while inside my new language and culture. I experienced changes in how I felt and acted and perceived myself as a white, Jewish-American woman. I became more aware that one is socialized into a culture through words, tone, and implicit understandings of one's place, and that there are penalties for people who violate the rules. Situated in between English and Japanese as I was, I suddenly had a unique vantage point to see structures in my own language and culture more clearly. Since the language (tone of voice and word choice) I was expected to use in different social contexts in Japan made me constantly aware of my status in relation to others, I became more sensitized to the many ways power mediates discourse exchanges. I was especially conscious of the role of gender in my language socialization process. This new consciousness was at once frightening and empowering, in that it gave me a sense of agency, a feeling that I had some choice of what to comply with and what I could actively resist. Although I focused on gender in my language-learning experiences, I clearly could not entirely isolate gender from other categories of identity.

The narratives in this book reflect this complex interplay between gender, social status, nationality, race, class, and language learning. More specifically, they focus on what happens to the self when exposed to an outside world of increasing diversity. The book is based on a theoretical framework loosely defined in applied linguistics research as Introspection. In this book the concept refers to looking at one's own language-learning experiences in light of the social, cultural, and political contexts in which they occur. Similar work can be found in diary studies (see Bailey, 1980; Ogulnick, 1999; Schmidt & Frota, 1986; Schumann, 1980) and the emerging literature of memoirs that deal with the impact the process of adapting to another language and culture has on one's sense of self (see Gilyard, 1991; Kaplan, 1994; Lvovich, 1997; Ogulnick, 1998).

Although self-reflection is an important starting point for getting at the root of some of our historical, psychological, and political existence, the optical metaphor in this work goes beyond simply looking at oneself to making visible that which has been overlooked. The feminist scientist Donna Haraway (2000, p. 103) uses the term *diffraction* to capture the more political process of breaking things down and casting light on the power of the everyday. Critical language theorists such as Bourdieu (1977), Foucault (1986), and Freire (1990) have focused on the ways structural power in society affect what people say and how they speak. This lens has helped us see that language is not neutral: The ways people interact—who controls and dominates the talk, whose meanings count, who authorizes what can be said and when and how—all these social, cultural, and political factors affect how people learn languages. They also help to explain the failure to learn languages, which often lead to considerable pain and regret. To be sure, linguistic autobiographies are rich fields to mine. Even more so than in other areas of learning, culturally determined relational patterns become revealed in the process of learning a language. Since the very act of writing autobiography shapes history and identity as much as the narratives are shaped by them, this work is ultimately about making a difference in the world.

Since all personal experience is subjective and all knowledge is partial, I took special care to include many different perspectives and to preserve the rhythm of the different voices as much as possible. When reading these texts, I thought of French poststructuralist writers such as Hélène Cixous, Julia Kristeva, and Luce Irigary, whose writing about language is closely bound to the body. Roland Barthes perhaps expressed the physicality of language most vividly when he said, "Language is a skin: I rub my language against the other. It is as if I had words instead of fingers, or fingers at the tip of my words" (quoted in Haraway, 2000, p. 86). As if taking Hélène Cixous's advice (which was addressed to women) to "Write yourself, your body must make itself heard" (1989, p. 116), many writers in this volume wrote to reclaim identities that have been masked by dominant cultures. They also used intensely physical metaphors to describe their pain, struggles, and feelings related to love, spirituality, and often of being contained in and shaped by the languages they were learning.

These vivid metaphors have not only been instructive, they were also helpful in creating an organizing framework. However, like languages and people themselves, the essays do not fit neatly into one category. For example, the first section, "Dislocations," deals with the tensions involved in moving from one linguistic culture to another. I placed essays here that focused on experiences of dislocation most directly; however, readers will find this theme in many other pieces as well. Other major themes in this book include how patterns of social and cultural behaviors (such as domination, control, and the impact of silence) are revealed in the process of language learning; how people negotiate their life experiences through different languages; how language relates to the ways people define their identities and maintain subcultures; and how the process of language learning interacts with psychological, emotional, sociocultural, and political realities.

As we step out of our understandings of everyday life, our familiarity in categorizing the world, and the rhythms we're accustomed to, our perspectives all of a sudden change. This creates a sense of dislocation. Ambiguities, contradictions, and ambivalences inherent in living in between cultures are revealed in the writers' explorations of how they negotiate the often disconnected realities of home and the larger community. Whether moving "from Bayamon to Brooklyn" (Maslanek), from Harlem to Queens (Sprott), or from Poland to Israel (Dykman), one's sense of identity and continuity gets short-circuited in a new physical and emotional environment. A person may feel uncomfortable at best and humiliated at worst, due to chauvinism built into cultural and linguistic boundaries. Even different climate and food can create feelings of dislocation. Many of these narratives, rooted in childhood, reveal the sharp observational skills of children who grew up as outsiders, as if they were "participant-observers" of their own lives, and exemplify the particular challenges the writers faced in later years as they confronted the outsider within. The pieces illustrate how the authors actively resisted subjugation and mistreatment through discourse practices (see Peirce, 1995; Weedon, 1987). The psychological implications and risks of negotiating a new existence are a strong theme of this section. The writers bring us on their often painful journeys into their new realities. Upon arrival, they enter new spaces of relocation, where they expand into their new experiences.

The social and cultural dislocations described in the previous section become even more pronounced in Part II, "Mother Tongues." The writers reveal the strong bonds that tie people to the languages of their parents, grandparents, and communities. The stories in this section bring to light the depth of commitment required to reconnect with linguistic roots that have been severed by the requirement of assimilation into the dominant culture, a message ubiquitously transmitted in schools, the workplace, and society. Theodore Roosevelt clearly articulated the sentiment of the times when he said, "We have room for but one language here, and that is the English language" (Nieto, 1996, p. 193). A sobering realization for many writers in this section is that as children they had internalized the denial and hatred spewed forth by this monocultural mandate.

The writers in Part III, "The Difficulties of Language Learning," describe socially caused inhibitions, whether they occurred in school settings, family, or through the confines of a culture. These moving pieces all reflect a feeling of regret that something good and important might have been taken away by attitudes and situations that made language learning an unpleasant experience. They clearly indicate that a framework of negative experiences destroys the potential for what could be so many positive ones.

In contrast to the difficulties described above, the pieces in Part IV, "Our Love Affairs with Languages: Stories of Multi-Language Learners," are all written by talented polyglots. A metaphor that I took to heart, which appears elsewhere in the book but comes through most prominently in this section, is the image of being in relationships—with all the complexity of feeling that underlies them. These individuals have embraced the opportunity to get inside languages, to be enveloped and enlarged by them. The ability to speak many languages gives these people more colorful, flavorful, expansive lives. Language learning opens them up not only to other cultures and ways of understanding the world, but ultimately to themselves, by providing a wider spectrum of feelings, thoughts, and ways of expressing their different personas in various languages.

In "Close Encounters with Other Cultures: Learning Language While Living Abroad," the writers describe their experiences learning foreign languages abroad. While sharing similarities to some of the perceptions described in "Dislocations," for these writers, being the "other" is often a temporary status. The outsider experience nevertheless provides these writers with new lenses through which they can see their own cultures more clearly and gain valuable insight into how they've been shaped by their particular language socialization processes.

In light of the current wave of anti-immigrant sentiment in the United States and around the world, as reflected in restrictive language legislation being proposed and passed, the complex interplay between language and identity cannot be ignored. Issues of cultural identity are being explored, debated, and focused on in this society. Regardless of whether we are multilingual or monolingual, one experience we all share is contact with languages, dialects, and cultures different from our own. New interpretive frameworks can help us respond to the nativist position that expresses intolerance to linguistic diversity. Respect, appreciation, and curiosity are basic elements in building the kinds of bridges that will enable us to get along in increasingly multicultural environments. While taking in these wondrous and diverse linguistic self-portraits, readers are invited to engage in a similar process of personal and cultural exploration. It is hoped that this contribution to the literature on introspection in language learning will inspire people to do so. We all have important stories to tell.

References

Bailey, K. (1980). An introspective analysis of an individual's language learning experience. In R. Scarcella & S. Krashen (Eds.), *Research in second language acquisition* (pp. 58–65). Rowley, MA: Newbury House.

Bourdieu, P. (1977). The economics of linguistic exchanges. *Social Science Information, 16*(6), 645–668.

Cixous, H. (1989). Sorties: Out and out: Attacks/ways out/forays. In C. Belsey & J. Moore (Eds.), *The feminist reader: Essays in gender and the politics of literacy criticism* (pp. 101–116). Cambridge, MA: Blackwell.

Foucault, M. (1986). *Language, counter-memory, practice: Selected essays and interviews.* Ithaca, NY: Cornell University Press.

Freire, P. (1990). *Pedagogy of the oppressed* (rev. ed.). New York: Continuum.

Gilyard, K. (1991). *Voices of the self: A study of sociolinguistic competence.* Detroit: Wayne State University Press.

Haraway, D. J. (2000). *How like a leaf.* New York: Routledge.

Kaplan, A. (1994). *French lessons: A memoir.* Chicago: University of Chicago Press.

Lvovich, N. (1997). *The multilingual self: An inquiry into language learning.* Mahwah, NJ: Lawrence Erlbaum.

Murray, D. (1990). *Shoptalk: Learning to write with writers.* Portsmouth, NH: Boynton/ Cook Heinemann.

Nieto, S. (1996). *Affirming diversity: The sociopolitical context of multicultural education.* New York: Longman.

Ogulnick, K. (1998). *Onna rashiku (Like a woman): The diary of a language learner in Japan.* Albany: State University of New York Press.

Ogulnick, K. (1999). Introspection as a method of raising critical language awareness. *The Journal of Humanistic Education, 37*(3), 145–159.

Peirce, B. N. (1995). Social identity, investment, and language learning. *TESOL Quarterly, 29*(1), 9–31.

Schmidt, R. W., & Frota, S. N. (1986). Developing basic conversational ability in a second language: A case study of an adult learner of Portuguese. In R. Day (Ed.), *Talking to learn: Conversation in second language acquisition* (pp. 237–326). Cambridge, MA: Newbury House Publishers.

Schumann, F. (1980). Diary of a language learner: A further analysis. In R. Scarcella & S. Krashen (Eds.), *Research in second language acquisition* (pp. 51–57). Rowley, MA: Newbury House.

Weedon, C. (1987). *Feminist practice and poststructuralist theory.* London: Basil Blackwell.

Part I

DISLOCATIONS

The writers in this opening section describe their spinning, shifting senses of themselves as they move inside various spaces, trying to maintain their dignity along the way. In the opening piece, Myrna Nieves uses the metaphor "puzzle" in a poem about writing in English, her second language. She captures the immigrant experience of fragmentation and imbalance at having to guess at meaning without having a complete picture. Greta Hofmann Nemiroff examines her trilingualism (German, English, French) in its complex political contexts. She discusses the affective and political ramifications of her attachment to German, her first language, as a child of Jewish Austrian parents who had the good fortune to immigrate to Quebec in 1929. She investigates the position of "other" to which language and ethnicity have always relegated her as a member of a minority within the English community in Montreal, which itself is a minority within the greater French community of Quebec. She traces the ways in which her use of language has always been mediated by politics, and she explores how this affects her. A Swiss immigrant to Montreal, Verena Stefan writes from the experience of broken languages, reflecting on how she perceives and assimilates new words and expressions and what exactly makes a foreign idiom speak to her. The process of immigration deconstructs her familiar "I," ultimately offering her the opportunity to literally change her mind while finding her way in two foreign languages. As a polyglot and a writer who prefers to see the world as a large home base, she comes to the conclusion that living in foreign languages means not only loss of identity, but also an abundance of language, stimulation, and change. Elizabeth Dykman's language and cultural awareness journey brings us from Poland to Israel, where she and her family migrated after enduring years of persecution for being Jewish. Her piece poignantly depicts the natural impulse people have to cross linguistic and cultural borders, even in the face of senseless bigotry. Rita Negron Maslanek, a Puerto Rican immigrant, also recalls early stigmatizing words used to cast her as an outsider. As a student, she quickly learned that she could dodge racist verbal assaults by being funny, which she achieved simply by asking a question or mispronouncing a word, especially when it annoyed her teachers. Maslanek discusses learning English during the pre-bilingual education era—otherwise known as "sink or swim" (see Ovando & Collier, 1998). Maslanek's strong affiliation to her church and her role as interpreter for her parents, as well as the "Spanish-only" rule at home, helped her to maintain her native language, which research indicates is a key predictor for academic success in a second language (Cummins, 1979, 1989; Nieto, 1996). While recognizing how traumatic English immersion can be for some, including her cousin, who said she was "scarred for life," Maslanek offers a thoughtful and respectful critique on bilingual education. Although I, a supporter of bilingual education, do not favor the English-immersion approach, I believe her cogent arguments are important to listen to. They provide ferment for discussion on the complexity of variables involved, such as individual differences, political controversy, and practical problems with the administration, design, and implementation of bilingual education programs (see Arias & Cosanova, 1993).

Several writers in this section focus specifically on dialectical variation, which is a salient issue not only for those learning other languages but also for many native speakers. With an estimated one-third of the U.S. population being immigrants by the middle of the 21st century, classrooms that were once considered bilingual are becoming increasingly multilingual. Along with this phenomenon is the inevitable variation of "Englishes" spoken in various linguistic communities both within and outside the United States. "World English" speakers have been designated the second-fastest-growing population of international students in the United States (Crandall, 1995). The ambiguity between language and dialect is powerfully expressed in Max Weinreich's (1945) metaphor: "A language is a dialect with an army and a navy" (trans-lated from "A shprakh is a diyalekt mit an armey un a flot"). Clearly, this distinction continues to blur as the world population migrates and national borders change.

Having experienced shame and obliteration of their native dialects due to the negative perceptions attached to them, it's no coincidence that the next three writers have all become teachers devoted to affirming linguistic and cultural diversity in their students. They give voice to the unique and creative qualities nonstandard forms of English may have. They illustrate how the dominant culture's rejection of a person's way of speaking may cause resistance to standard forms as well as internalized rejection of one's own language. By imposing a form that may be inhibiting, the culture may confine a person within his or her perceived limits. These writers, as well as many others, provide testament to the powerful connections native dialects call up to the voices of one's parents, grandparents, and communities. Elizabeth Nuñez, born in Trinidad, recalls being taught that her imaginative renderings of a world she did not know (England) had more value than her realistic portrayal of her own world. She finds the same phenomenon to be true in her students from Caribbean and African countries, who often use their speaking voices for telling the truth, and their writing voices for concealing the truth behind false words and sentence structures. Ruby Sprott, an African American woman, focuses on language learning through the lenses of race and gender. She reflects on her experiences of being restricted at school and often at home to expressions in standard English, which she found confining in many ways. Raimundo Mora, who moved from Ecuador to Colombia and then to New York as a young adult, addresses language and dialect shifts in Spanish and English, what he has learned about the relationship between identity and literacy, and how it informs his teaching of young adult English language learners.

References

Arias, B., & Casanova, U. (Eds.). (1993). *Bilingual education: Politics, practice, research.* Chicago, IL: University of Chicago Press.

Crandall, J. (1995). Reinventing (America's) schools: The role of the applied linguist. In J. E. Alatis (Ed.), *Linguistics and the education of language teachers: Ethnolinguistic, psycholinguistic, and sociolinguistic aspects* (pp. 413–427). Washington, DC: Georgetown University Press.

Cummins, J. (1979). Linguistic interdependence and the educational development of bilingual children. *Review of Educational Research, 49,* 222–251.

Cummins, J. (1989). *Empowering minority students.* Sacramento, CA: California Association for Bilingual Education.

Nieto, S. (1996). *Affirming diversity: The sociopolitical context of multicultural education.* New York: Longman.

Ovando, C., & Collier, V. (1998). *Bilingual and ESL classrooms: Teaching in multicultural contexts.* New York: McGraw-Hill.

Weinreich, M. (1945). *Der yevo un di problem en fun undzer tsayt.* [YIVO and the problems of our time.] *YIVO-bleter.*

Puzzle

MYRNA NIEVES

I do not know
why am I writing in English
a second language
a wave where
spaces open into a void
and you just need
to jump off a cliff

A language where approximate sounds
suggest what I would like to say
A language with blanks
—like in a test—
which my memory will fill
sometime in the future.

No Language to Die In

GRETA HOFMANN NEMIROFF

Ur

Although I was born in the linguistically divided city of Montréal in 1937, my first language was neither French nor English, it was German. My Viennese parents and grandmother also spoke the Viennese dialect (*"Wienerisch"*), depending on the emotional tone of the occasion. Every morning of my early childhood I would run across the hall to my grandmother Malvine's bed where she had confected a little corner (*"eine kleine Ecke"*) for me within the puffs and undulations of featherbeds and eiderdowns, whose covers were generously embroidered and edged in lace—relics of her trousseau, sewn when she was a young woman "in waiting." Malvine told me enchanting stories in German about waltzing the nights away at grand balls in the Vienna of the *Belle Époque*. I preferred her tales of the monkeys' antics in the ornate Affenhaus at the Schöenbrunn Palace Zoo. Sometimes she would read me *"Maerchen,"* fairy tales by the Brothers Grimm or Hans Christian Andersen, from books written in the old Germanic script and illustrated with exquisitely detailed and sometimes terrifying steel engravings. I loved tracing the mysterious f's, s's, and k's with my forefinger as I lay safe within the circle of her softness and warmth, scornful of the winter raging right outside our window.

Malvine did not speak English, nor did she have to; she negotiated her way successfully around Montréal in very good French, which she had learned in Vienna. When I was seven, Malvine died right after a triumphant VE day. I was never to speak German so consistently again; my most active vocabulary remains locked within the minutiae of a childhood in a well-run household.

Language Crossings: Negotiating the Self in a Multicultural World. Copyright © 2000 by Teachers College, Columbia University. All rights reserved. ISBN 0-8077-3998-7 (pbk.), ISBN 0-8077-3999-5 (cloth). Prior to photocopying items for classroom use, please contact the Copyright Clearance Center, Customer Service, 222 Rosewood Dr., Danvers, MA 01923, USA, tel. (508) 750-8400.

I inherited Malvine's room, but it was already stripped of the faint scent of chamomile and lavender. Malvine's stories and fairy tales were superseded by the intrigues of Angela Brazil's British schoolgirls and the adventures of the rebellious Susannah of the Mounties, whom I emulated.

German is my "ur-language." Woven into the configuration of my mind, it encompasses those verbal fragments and expressions that evoke my earliest and even some preverbal memories. It touches on my deepest emotions. My sister and I still interlace our English conversation with German expressions because they provide the most accurate configuration of qualities suited to our meanings. Like Malvine and our mother, Lisl, we use the adjective *"unappetitlich"* ("unappetizing") not only to describe food, but also to describe dirty surroundings, unclean clothes and bed linens, and morally or physically "soiled" individuals. *"Gemeinheit"* not only suggests meanness and ill will, but also encompasses the motivation for acts of intentional cruelty. Living in a post-Holocaust consciousness, I am not surprised that this word is not fully translatable from the German. There is a lexicon of German words that informs my speech during those increasingly rare times when I am in the company of German-speakers.

German is the language of those dreams that emerge from my early childhood; it also springs to my tongue when I am in pain or when something in nature is *"wunderschöen"* ("wonderfully beautiful"). The structures of the language are so embedded in my speech that I am often surprised by the appearance of Germanic sentence structure in the first drafts of my written work or in my spontaneous speech. I am troubled that I can still find it so comforting to hear the soft Austrian German or Viennese dialect spoken by strangers. I feel obliged to stop myself short by recalling the twistings, turnings, and opportunistic revisions cobbled together by postwar Austrians when confronted by evidence of their enthusiastic welcome of National Socialism in 1938. Within the soft glow of my ur-German lies the hard comprehension that had my parents not been willing to relinquish home and mother tongue in 1929, I would not have made it past even the "first selection" for the gas chambers.

By the time my mother died in 1978, her German-speaking friends had already died or moved away. I wanted to write a letter announcing her death to her family in Austria. Since my written German is not good, I contacted a German colleague to help me. In the course of our conversation, he mentioned quite casually that as a child in Austria he had been a member of the Hitler Jugend (Hitler Youth). Although the irony of the situation escaped neither of us, we did not pursue this painful subject. Where could such a discussion carry people who are obliged to work together?

My German is a fragmented ur-language locked in my heart and only sometimes released to my tongue, shard by shard. The passage from heart to tongue is arduous, burdened by the ambiguities of love and history as well as mistakes in grammar and inflection. My tongue often feels rusty, and the words then come slowly, bridging the interruptions of time and place. At its best, it overflows with the preserved memories of those whose world has irrevocably vanished with them, the *mittel*-European emigré(e)s whose knowledge, humor, and love suffused my Montréal childhood with light.

Aenglisch, English, Anglophone

I was always "good" in English. As a child I was an insatiable reader; I won writing prizes in school, university, and later. I hold university degrees in English literature, which I have taught in colleges and universities for 36 years. I have written, edited, and published numerous articles, stories, and books. I have served on editorial boards of learned and popular journals, and I have been in demand as a public speaker. Barring my very first words, I have spoken English almost as long as I have spoken German. I maintain common-place books in which I copy English texts that have especially touched or pleased me. How is it, then, that I do not feel a profound or truly affectionate bond with the language? It slides in and out of me with fluency and style, but it is detached from my deepest affective life.

If German inhabits my body, English clothes me in a well-tailored and somewhat elegant costume. Often I dream in English; I speak it with my children, at work, and with many of my friends. It has been the currency of expression with lovers and a then-husband. It works for me in numerous contexts, but I do not dare get too attached to it, since I have been constructed as an "other" both within and because of it.

My identity as an English-speaking Québecker (since 1976 we have been officially called "anglophones") is the result of distant adventures, battles, treaties, and legislative acts of European men. After the British conquest of Québec in 1759, until 1998, children's access to public education was determined by language and religion. The Catholic school systems were divided between English and French schools; "others" attended Protestant schools, which until fairly recently were all English. The Protestant School Board of Greater Montréal of the 1930s–1960s was controlled primarily by Protestants of British or Scottish extraction. These stalwarts undertook the task of socializing *all* children in their school system into a slightly distorted proto-British stance filtered through a loose mesh of Scottish Presbyterianism. During World War II, we children sang from a buff-colored songbook, inspiring bewildering tears to the adults' eyes with our renditions of "The Bluebells of Scotland," "My Bonnie Lies Over the

Ocean," and "The Maple Leaf Forever." I barely bothered to learn the words to these songs; I comprehended that these were someone else's stories, and that this "someone else" neither liked me nor had my best interests at heart.

Ironically, the social and institutional anti-Semitism inherent in Québec's English school system at the time was one of the elements that shaped my fragile Jewish identity, since I was brought up in a totally secular household. Our high school math teacher unselfconsciously sniffed disdainfully at the presence in the school of a "certain element," referring to children of the numerous Jewish families who had moved to our middle-class district, Notre-Dame-de-Grace. I then attended McGill University, which had a quota for Jewish students in several faculties well into the 1960s. The message that as a Jew I was accepted only under sufferance was not a propitious environment for cultural bonding.

While I went through the necessary motions for admission to the Québec anglophone world, it was a stuggle not to reject the culture, a dangerous transplantation of an essential organ. While I read, appreciated, and wrote about the "classics," I was puzzled by the professors' claims of their universality. Were the most "universal themes" love and war as sung by Virgil in the opening lines of *The Aeneid*? Was Keats's Grecian urn, a circle depicting the "complementary" themes of rape and death, really a universal image demonstrating that "beauty is truth, truth beauty?" Later, feminist and critical analytic tools helped me to unravel the knots created by such blithe and jingoistic claims. I came to understand that the primary purpose of my "liberal arts" education had been to maintain the hegemony of male European culture.

As a non-Catholic child born in Québec, I am an "anglophone" by default. History has created a minority-of-a-minority context for my speech. Considering the options facing Viennese Jews of my generation, I have been extremely fortunate. Both of my parents achieved modest success within the English-speaking community, and I have benefited from their labors in difficult times.

As with my German identity, my English one is fraught with ambiguity and ambivalence. By the time I was an adult, the "Quiet Revolution" of the French majority was under way. Whether or not all francophones wanted to separate from the rest of Canada, there was a consensus that Québec was not to be bilingual; French was legislated as the official language. Children of immigrants were to assimilate through enforced attendance at French schools; language laws on advertising, business communication, and the Internet were created to enforce the dominance of French over "other languages" and to counter the hegemony of English in North America. A government agency was formed to promote French and to enforce the language laws.

While I am fluent in French, it is nonetheless painful to experience the enforced invisibility of English, a language grafted onto me and diligently learned. Moreover, the language of English-speaking Québeckers is filled with French expressions. Translators of my work into French often complain that my English is so full of French expressions that it is difficult to translate my work into French.

More difficult, however, has been the recognition that the French majority relegates me to the position of "other," as a member of the very anglophone community that initially defined me as "other," as a Jew. Since so many English-speaking Québeckers have defected to more clement environments since the laws of 1976, the very people who had only grudgingly let me into some of their institutions in the past now need people like me to inflate their ever-diminishing power base. New generations of immigrants to Québec, educated in French institutions, do not necessarily identify with the situation of the old English-speaking community. English rights groups, heavily subsidized by the federal government, claim to be protecting my interests, although I have given them no such mandate. I must admit to a certain glee at the spectacle of the once blithely powerful scrambling for toeholds and niches in the new order. In this context of anglophone hypocrisy, I celebrate the arbitrary nature of my linguistic formation, the shallowness of its roots, and the skills acquired over a lifetime of mediating its ever-shifting ambiguities.

Allophone, Francophone, Québécoise

Like many Europeans of their time and social class, my parents believed that multilingualism was indispensable for both survival and cultural enrichment. (Both of them had learned French in school in Austria; were they alive today, they would be surprised to discover that people like them are now officially defined as "allophones," while their children, forced into the English community, are called "anglophones.") Our maid, Marie-Ange, was a unilingual francophone from the Gaspésie; I was a flower girl at her wedding. I cannot remember not understanding French, and I enjoy speaking it. My written French, however, is awkward even when it is grammatically correct. If German resides within the marrow of my bones and English is a well-designed costume, French is the light outergarment that enhances my appearance and provides protection in inclement weather.

As an adolescent, I fell deeply in love with postwar France and its mythology of civic and moral courage. This was communicated to me through the songs and writings of Piaf, Greco, Montand, Prévert, de Beauvoir, Sartre, and Camus. The French existentialists seduced me with their contents and their language. Draped in black from head to toe, I hung around artists' cafés in Montréal listening to Piaf regretting nothing ("*Non, je ne regrette rien!*").

I was also enchanted by the exquisite rendering of French alexandrines in the classics brought from Paris to Montréal by the Barrault-Renaud theatre company. A passionate francophile, I longed to speak in a French as precise and musical as theirs and tried to force it through calcified layers of German and English.

One day in graduate school in Boston, I overheard two young men speaking Québec French in the library. My heart ached with homesickness as they reported that things were changing in Québec. I returned to the "Quiet Revolution" and realized that if I wanted to participate fully in this emerging society, I must perfect my French. I spent two years under the tutelage of Mademoiselle Provencher, a retired translator and maiden lady with impeccable antecedents in Montréal society. My family spent 15 summers in the totally francophone Comté Labelle, where we enjoyed the friendship of three generations of the St. Jean family, local farmers. It was in their kitchen that my understanding of Québec culture deepened well beyond language.

My former attachment to France was replaced by an intense interest in the French around me, especially those writers like the playwright Michel Tremblay, who infused his language with the vernacular "joual," and the reappropriation of the language by feminist writers such as Marie-Claire Blais, Jovette Marchessault, and Louky Bersianik. The "Quiet Revolution" transformed me from a francophile to a Québécophile, even though I was aware that old-stock francophone Québécois still referred to themselves as "*nous autres*" (we others) and to the non-francophone Québeckers as "*vous autres*" (you others).

In 1970 I became active in the creation of the community college system in Québec and negotiated English literature curriculum over ten years. This work regularly took me to the capital, Québec City, where I was obliged to decode the educational and philosophical assumptions of colleagues who shared a fairly homogeneous vision, having been educated in francophone institutions run by various religious orders. Often after a day or two of meetings, I would experience painful headaches and burning eyes. Language would freeze in midsentence on my tongue. I, who err on the side of volubility, would be forced into silence until words could slowly trickle back.

This silence was not a result of poor vocabulary. It was produced by the stress of having to counter the assumptions inherent in my being inaccurately identified with the opinions of the anglophone "other." It is difficult to have coherent and consequent discussion while correcting the assumptions of others. At best I have been granted the position of an "exotic other," labeled such by the opacity of my three non-English names. Often when I have given a talk in French some member of the audience will ask me, "What are your origins, *Madame*?" This need to "place" me is not meant to harm me; rather, it reflects the current politics of language in Québec.

Although the linguistic truths about me are fraught with many political complexities, I usually offer this short and somewhat ingenuous answer: "I was born in Montréal." What I do not usually add, however, is that although I cannot produce a grandmother from St-Pie-de-Bagot, a grandfather from Glasgow, or even a parent from a *stetl* in Galicia, I am nonetheless a Québécoise. I have learned French and Québec culture through inclination, not through legislation. Moreover, while I resent the fact that this "otherness" has been imposed upon me by the imperialistic ambitions of warring groups of anti-Semitic elite European men centuries ago, I prefer my "otherness" to identifying with them. Ultimately, I celebrate the richness and diversity otherness has brought me, along with the opportunity for solidarity with other "others" in the world. *Tant pis; j'y suis et j'y reste* (Too bad; I'm here and I'm staying!).

No Language to Die In

Conflicts regarding minority language entitlements abound throughout officially bilingual Canada. The fact that the languages of Canada's aboriginal peoples are not included in this formula is a clear sign of the invidious status accorded to them by the European invaders. Much of the conflict is manifested by the struggle of minority groups (anglophones in Québec and francophones in other provinces) for access to social, health, and educational services in their mother tongues. In and out of Québec, minority groups have been able to rally strong public support for the right to die in one's first language. Public opinion can be powerfully stirred by accounts of suffering people unable to make their desperate needs known to health care professionals while dying in excruciating pain.

As I age, I find myself riveted by journalistic accounts of this predicament. I have wondered in which language I should utter my last pained requests. I know that if I were to use German, I would have great difficulty. An emergency visit to a doctor in Salzburg some years ago reduced me to the undignified position of using the word "peepee" to explain symptoms of cystitis, a urinary infection. My childhood kitchen vocabulary is simply not up to it. I can acquit myself honorably in English, but in Québec I might die in the hands of unilingual francophones. I am therefore glad to report that some years ago, after an automobile accident, the ambulance attendant engaged me in conversation to keep me conscious. When he left me at the hospital, he congratulated me on the fluency of my French. I had not realized that I was speaking French.

While it might be comforting to die in my most deeply felt language, I have no choice. I cannot die in German and must resort to my secondary and tertiary languages. The language of the heart and the language of expediency will have to work separately at this crucial defining moment. Be that is it may, I am not worried; I can die in peace where I was born.

3

Here's Your Change 'N Enjoy the Show

VERENA STEFAN

Heimatort—Place of Origin

I grew up in a house of shy and broken languages. My mother was Swiss German and therefore learned the "High" German of Germany as a second language, French as a third, and English as a fourth. Swiss German and High German exemplify two different systems of language. German people don't understand or speak Swiss German. In the German part of Switzerland we grow up with two languages: Swiss German and the German of school, literature, the media, and bureaucracy.

My mother's French was mediocre, as was her English. She had little practice in these languages and felt shy speaking them. Her fifth language, the written one, she kept hidden in secret notebooks all her life. My father's knowledge of French and English was poor, and he felt rather embarrassed to speak them. His mother tongue was German. Since he came from the German-speaking part of Czechoslovakia, his first broken language was Czech.

In Switzerland each child learns in first grade that there is a place of origin, a *Heimatort. Heimat* is a fundamental word in the German language, meaning at the same time home, native country, and any place where one feels at home geographically, emotionally, or mentally. In Switzerland it is defined by the Constitution that one's community of origin is obliged to take care of you if you don't have the means to do so due to illness or old age. Therefore Swiss children learn the name of their place of origin by heart so they will know where they belong. I made a stunning discovery in the first grade: I had no place of origin, because my father was Sudetendeutsch, from the small town of Maehrisch-Ostrau. Switzerland is not a country of immigration. The law of the fathers says that his place of origin is vaild for the whole family. I lived in my mother's village, in her parent's house, spoke her Bernese language and had no place of origin.

Whenever it was my turn at school to announce it, the teacher intervened, telling me: "You don't need to say your place of origin, there is something wrong with you." What she said (*mit dir stimmt etwas nicht*) would literally mean, "You don't fit in." I remained silent, with a locked-up tongue. A foreign tongue lay upon my tongue and I longed to say out loud the foreign, intriguing name Maehrisch-Ostrau. I loved its sound, which carried a secret, something that was not correct, that was far away "in the East," hidden behind an Iron Curtain.

The incident at elementary school remained a crucial element throughout my life, with varying consequences. I learned: The maternal place of origin is not valid because the law promotes the paternal one. One mustn't say that publicly. Home, feeling at home, and knowing where I belong were unmentionable. Top secret.

Since then, the unmentionable and I belong together. Apart from that, I do not know where I belong. So far my fundamental urge has been to mention the unmentionable; writing is the main locus for it. By unearthing a hitherto unmentionable issue, I create a textual body and provide a place where I belong.

It seemed easy for me in my mid-twenties to endorse Virginia Woolf's (1966) statement: "As a woman I have no country. As a woman I want no country. As a woman my country is the whole world" (p. 109). I lived in Berlin from 1968 to 1975 and stayed in Germany for 30 years as a permanent resident. I never applied for citizenship. I became a leftist, a feminist, a lesbian, a writer living in the High German tongue of the written word in a then-split city in the middle of a forbidden zone.

Polyglots—*Polies Glottes*—Friendly Tongues

Thirty years later I find myself in a bilingual city on another continent, in Montréal. Is a *leap of faith* the same as *un acte de foi*? Are there immigration laws here? Yes, there are many, so many people can immigrate. *The days are packed*, this I learned from *Calvin & Hobbes*. Sensations, sounds, sights, words. Words words words. What is the true word for . . . how would you say in English—*comment dirait-on en français*? My ears, my body are filled with noise. English and French words come back to me through books, magazines, radio, conversations with friends, memories of the 1988 International Feminist Book Fair at Montréal.

"Do you sometimes feel like an object moving through space?" a friend asks. "I'm out on a limb," I answer, trying an idiom I have read somewhere. "This is dangerous," she says, fixing me seriously with her eyes. I am baffled. I don't feel as if I am in a dangerous situation or in a questionable state of mind yet. I wanted to try that expression. Out-on-a-limb sent a stretching sensation through my arms so that they seemed to touch the unknown more easily. What did I want to tell her? That I was ready to go to the ends of the world to change? That I felt again like a polyglot globetrotter, setting off for a three-month trip to the North American continent, as I did once before in my life, back in 1974? That I felt at home in the transience of moving around in an airport between two stops, everybody else around me being in transition as well? The normal status of people in airports: not to be at home. Not to belong. Not knowing whether one will arrive at the point of destination. A couple of hours in the middle of nowhere, only the very necessary things on my back: notebook, pen, computer, passport, traveler's checks, address book, cash, colored pencils, books to read, camera, toiletries, reading glasses. (On the following trips, also a thin folder with all the necessary documents to prove that I am the person immigration authorities might want to know I am.) That I liked to dislocate myself with my mobile office on my body, my portable identity, from one place to another? That I felt free to move, to talk, to write, to present myself as if attending an international conference? That I liked the idea of moving as far out as I could on a branch of a tree, like I did as a kid? Language is visceral. Having felt how she held her breath in reaction to my remark, I keep a nuanced perception of "out-on-a-limb." (*Better beat a hasty retreat*, I haven't stored in my repertoire yet.)

At first it is very pleasant not to have an identity anymore. *As happy as a clam.* There are no friends, former lovers, blood relatives, colleagues, or little dogs who know me. I have to concentrate fully on my third and fourth languages and forget my habitual verbal patterns. The German verb for "translate" is *übersetzen*, which means both to set off from one shore to another (originally, being transported in a rowboat by a ferryman), and to transfer text from one language into another. Setting off from one continent and landing on another therefore means to translate myself, my whole existence into another one, without knowing the target language.

I read English and French books with dictionaries. If I don't (because I simply want to read a book as usual, as if I didn't need dictionaries), I read with two minds, the second mind telling the first one: save *brim over, redolent with lavender, pediment, impediment, detriment, gossamer wing*; and look up later: *jetty, thudding, callous, unsheathe, squeamish, désarçonné* (abashed), *mon coeur allait se rompre á force de cogner* (my heart was going to burst, it was beating so hard).

This is excellent brain training, I keep telling myself, especially at age 50. But after having overadapted for many months, I am worn out and at the lowest of my emotional and spiritual energy. My being-in-progress doesn't have a body yet in the new languages, maybe a bit of an English body, but almost no French textual body. No feet, no bones, no muscles. The words haven't reached body temperature yet as in writing, when every word of the text to come has to assume one's body temperature to become fully alive. For example, take *Forhereortogo?* It took me several times until I understood this simple question in a coffee shop. I call it the "banal split second," telling the salesperson twice or three times: "I-don't-understand forhereortogo." On good days I might add, "Could you repeat it slower, please? You're talking too fast for me." I might even say, "*Would you mind being so kind* as to repeat it slower?" With these requests, I rearrange my situation, lifting the weightiness of the foreigner's confessional "I-don't-understand." Communication calls for a contribution of all involved. On bad days I don't understand any *forhereortogos.*

The first time I fully followed the above mumbled Longword, I felt another split-second reaction in my body that tongue-tied me, this time not being able to make a decision. For here? No, I don't want to drink my coffee in this coffee shop. I want to take it with me and place it in the cup holder of the rusty Chevy. I want to perform being in North America. I am European. But I want to stay *here* in North America, I don't want to *go* back to Germany. So I want my coffee "for to go," and I want to stay here, and most of all I want to get going. But *what's going on is not what's really happening.*

I perceive and receive language viscerally, visually, in homonyms, and symbolically. *Here's-your-change-and-enjoy-the-show* is another Longword I didn't understand the first time, after having paid for my movie ticket. I also didn't understand it due to a foreign, daily coded language of politeness, friendliness, and good humor. I don't expect the cashier to wish me to enjoy the movie. Nowhere in Germany or Switzerland would this ever happen to you. We are not used to the pursuit of happiness and take it for granted to choose whether we want to be happy or unhappy. We have the right to be unhappy or to be lost in fathomless brooding that leaves no space for friendliness. Neither habitual unfriendliness nor compulsory happiness work anyway. But I liked this sentence and thought I might as well try enjoying *my* show.

Crossings

I sit on an improvised bench inside an installation at the National Art Gallery in Ottawa. Viewers had to walk a long way down a meandering corridor that led through increasing darkness. At the beginning was one of the huge windows of the museum overlooking the park. In the maze, first you heard music and then you saw a tiny room with a virtual window overlooking Moscow's Red Square. A board on two paint buckets served as a bench. A big old radio on the floor released Russian chants. Green paint went halfway up one wall. The Russian artist was attempting to create a room, to install a new self somewhere. I understand the language of that installation immediately. There is no need for translation.

The window at the end of the corridor inside the maze opened into a dreamlike surreal view embracing subtextual life. I sat there for quite a while, staring out that inner window, listening to Russian music. It felt familiar. I felt at home, though I have never traveled to Russia. But I know exactly where it is: in the East. I know Russian music from records and radio, from films, and I know what it embraces: the Russian soul. Longing, melancholia, pathos, exile, suffering. Passion, endurance. Patience. Mighty far-reaching voices and melodies, crossing the void of the Russian landscape. Here, in the museum in Ottawa, I know little of what lies east, what lies west. East and West have become completely unfamiliar entities.

Trois-Rivières, Chicoutimi, Baie St.-Jacques . . . these names don't speak to me. Belgrade, Niš, Novi Sad, Priština, Skopje do. I know where they are, and a little bit of what they look like.

Bic, Rimouski, Kouchibouguac are names of places east of where I am now to which I have an emotional and geographical reference. But those names don't evoke "East" as I learned the word "East": that which was separated from the West, hidden, riddled with land mines. Forbidden. East is where one cannot go easily; there are borders, iron curtains, controls. Everything is literally out of proportion. Before I came here, there was an agreement of architecture, streets, vegetation, travel distances, all distances with my body, my emotions, my perception of the world. All of the above ingredients formed a net of orientation and mobility. Everything seemed tuned in, seemed proportional for decades. Then it all became too dense, narrow, suffocating.

I am driving on a dirt road now, lost between woods. The width of the road and the distance to the horizon are unknown to me. I have to learn a new language of proportions, of river and stream, of space and spaciousness, of the seasons, plants, and animals as well as of architecture and culture. Staring in rapture at *Le Fleuve* at Bic, once in summer, once in winter, listening to the clicking slushing sounds of small ice floes being pulled toward the ocean, the tides already pulling the water. With one breath I feel I will never have to go back to the density of Germany; with the next breath months later I feel forlorn. Enclosed by woods. An adopted child. Learning the world new, like a child. I am not situated in space yet; I am not even landing anymore. I am lost, missing the familiar language of European cultivated landscape, the beauty of the architecture and the carefree command of Swiss and German tongues. When I come to realize fully the absence of an evident body of language, the absence hits me with phantom pain. What an ordeal. I am keeping a record. I keep trying my word. Poetry remains reliable, offering a language I understand anywhere in the world. My favorite sign on the highway driving out of Montréal says LA PRAIRIE–NEW YORK and brings back an Emily Dickinson line to my mind: *To make a prairie it takes a clover and one bee* (1993, p. 134). For months I thought La Prairie meant the Western Prairies instead of simply being a Montréal suburb. La Prairie–New York encompassed all too well corny European assumptions we still treasure of Amerika! Amerika!

Falling

"*If it is a question of falling,*" Monique Wittig and Sande Zeig tell us in *Lesbian Peoples: Material for a Dictionary* (1979), "better to do it into the arms of one's companion lover, forward or backward, with eyes open or closed," (p. 53). German-speaking people don't like to fall, it seems. There is no equivalent in German for *falling in love* or *tomber amoureuse*. You are either in love or *amoureuse*, and you may choose between going to bed with her or sleeping with her, but there is no way to *make* love, *de faire l'amour*, and then *de faire un rêve*, to "make" a dream instead of just having a dream.

Falling in love, I am landing long before I will be applying for landing papers. I exhale, falling in love. Then I land in my physical body again, re-connecting with it as with an old lover I have neglected due to my mission to create new bodies of language. As always, at least one other dimension opens its reality to those falling in love, but this time I experience an extra sensation and relief from being in rapture and not needing words in the first place. There is body language, talkative eyes, lips tongues hands feet legs. Whole heads telling tales, backs, breasts, vulvas. The many tongues of sighing moaning breathing laughing yelling take over and luckily enough are communicating without the possible difficulties any two lesbian lovers might experience.

What a relief to express myself in a first language again, not to search constantly for precise words. No more translation needed here than any lovers need to translate from one universe to another.

My beloved one is Québécoise, with an Irish mother and a French-Canadian father. She moves with equal ease in both languages. Since we met first in English, it remains our first common tongue.

Words of course enter the picture quickly. And since my whole body is talking, they find landing places, too. (A very simple example would be: Kiss is close to *Kuss*, arm is *Arm*, breasts are *brüsten* and nipples—there is no German word for nipples, only a term that lacks any erotic implication: *Brustwarzen*-breastwarts. Yes, mind the Germans, the Swiss and the Austrians.)

My voice drops. It is falling, falling back into me. It seems to become possible, to re-voice myself in foreign tongue. Finally there are not only words and words piling up inside me anymore, but a whole language that develops from within my body.

Yielding

"Yield," for instance, is a word I couldn't get ahold of for a long time. It reminded me of "yell," and I mixed it up with "yearn," until the day a writer in New Mexico explained it to me in the following way: *Cats yield more to the bodies they are pressed against than dogs.* At that instant her cat was lying on a sunny spot behind a glass wall, leaning against an abandoned animal skeleton from the desert. Since then I understand *Yield to arriving traffic*, thinking it makes perfect sense to give way to other cars rather than to press mine against them. *Milosevic fléchit.* The war in Kosovo reaches me with words that don't speak to me. *Une flèche* is an arrow. But *Milosevic fléchit* means he submits. Does this mean he is yielding, still pressing the Yugoslavian Federation against the Republic of Kosovo?

I read *Le Devoir*, a francophone daily Montréal newspaper, occasionally, German and Swiss newspapers regularly on the Internet and sometimes at the Goethe Institute, I listen to the Canadian Broadcasting Corporation daily, I watch French- and English-Canadian and American TV at friends' houses frantically. *L'OTAN*, French for NATO, is one of many words that don't speak to me, it is an unfamiliar series of letters that don't evoke feelings of NATO bombing. I react to "human targets"—*menschliche schilde*—but not to *cibles vivantes*. The news from this atrocious war remains abstract and distant, even in English. I am filled with disgust, listening to the way broadcasting refers to some faraway country as "over there," over the ocean. I understand chagrin, chagrined, bereaved immediately and my heart fills with exactly those emotions. Does anybody here know how beautiful Kosovo is, all of Yugoslavia? How its languages sing in your ears? During a show on CBC Radio one of NATO's numerous accidents is mentioned, a bomb hitting a line of fleeing refugees. *The pilot dropped the bomb in good faith*, as did the pilot over Hiroshima. I have come to realize that there are whole sentences and specific expressions from this war I don't know in German. I didn't experience them and learn them in German; I learned them here. For there is a perverse distorted language of propaganda imposed on all of us with *humanitarian bombing* and *collateral damage*.

Changing

My *I* is hidden in a language almost nobody knows here, nobody speaks. That is to say, the old I, the somebody I was familiar with, is fading in an unspoken language. Is there anybody?

I love Montréal. I am delighted to live in a place with two main languages, though they are languages in conflict. Every time I come back from the States, I feel relieved to live in a place where English doesn't dominate, where I may go back and forth between English and French in the same sentence, taking as many words from each language as I need to communicate my issues. Questions of translation, different mentalities, oppression through language, and lost and recuperated voices are very present in everyday Montréal life.

French is not visceral to me. I am not equipped yet with the everyday small talk, nor with the specific vocabulary of the arts, of linguistics, politics, economics, and I am even further away from contributing anecdotes and jokes. My voice is stretched; it is high-pitched in an unfamiliar and unpleasant way, as if it were located outside of my body. When I speak French, I don't do it from my guts. Now and then my back starts aching at francophone gatherings. I notice a polite attentive expression on the faces around me when I start talking and sense impatient energy from the locals, who don't want to interrupt their storytelling too long.

"It took me two years to understand Québécois fully,"an anglophone immigrant writer tells me, "and four years to understand that I would never be capable to fully take part in an animated Québécois discussion."

I feel normal the very second she passes the information on to me. She's been living in Montréal for more than 25 years. A tremendous relief fills my body. My spine relaxes. At a francophone writers meeting I saw somebody without a voice, with a painful expression on his face for hours. It told of a far too stretched attention span, of emotional insecurity, of feeling awkward in his skin. He was one of the guest writers and he didn't speak French. I saw him shrinking into nobody by the hour, since he couldn't make proof of his existence, his thinking, by naming it. Therefore he found himself in a low feminine status. His posture and gestures spoke of confinement, of not-reaching-far-out, of not-taking-a-stand, of the stress of being excluded and wanting to belong. The tension between his very virile appearance and his weak social position was striking. Apart from that, I saw a human being stripped of language and suffering torments.

It is amazing what happens as soon as one takes the decision to change status, to become an immigrant, not to be a visitor, a traveler anymore. It happens overnight. There is a force, an influence, that is stronger than my desire to perceive the world at large as a vast home base and myself as a polyglot moving through it. Though I am still in a mostly white Western feminist quite lesbian world, though I am known as a writer and even get work here and there through Goethe Institutes and German departments of universities, though I once co-translated *The Dream of a Common Language* and *Lesbian Peoples: Material for a Dictionary*, there is something bigger than all of the above taken together grabbing me and dismembering me.

Will you accept me? I keep asking the new country. I ask, I apply. Will I pass? As whom? I have to prove that I am acceptable. After those decades of feminist debating, questioning, fighting against preconceived identities and muted female voices in the world, identity is falling apart again. My notion of identity, of an *I*, doesn't become questionable; it is out of the question. Would the right word be *jeopardized*? What ferocious animal is lying in ambush to attack identity? The question of the I, even the female I, in the world seems irrelevant as long as the immigrant non-I is taking over, deconstructing it completely. At the bottom layer of deconstruction I anticipate relief. The experience is just human. Additional identity labels like *feminist* or *lesbian* are superfluous.

Identities are boring. Nation-states are boring. Languages are interesting. Language itself, modeling and refining language from inside out, is most interesting. In a world of more than one language, there is language in abundance. There is stimulation in abundance to literally change my mind. Given the chance to change one's style, the habitual way of thinking, the grammatical structure, I take the opportunity to change my writing and therefore my nature. *I grew up in a house of shy and broken languages*, I wrote at the beginning of this text, and I already no longer know how to translate this sentence into German. I would have to write it entirely differently in German to begin with, and right now I wouldn't know how. It has slipped my mind, yielding to something to come.

Acknowledgments. I wish to thank Greta Hofmann Nemiroff and Lise Moisan for language counseling and stimulating discussions.

References

Dickinson, E. (1993). To make a prairie it takes a clover and one bee. *The collected poems of Emily Dickinson.* New York: Barnes & Noble.
Wittig, M., & Zeig, S. (1979). *Lesbian peoples: Material for a dictionary.* New York: Avon.
Woolf, V. (1966). *Three guineas.* New York: Harcourt Brace Jovanivich.

4

The Vagabond Years

ELIZABETH DYKMAN

Until the age of five I took it for granted that language comes with being. I assumed that everyone was just like me, speaking the same language and doing the same things. My awareness of language as a distinct phenomenon was developed by a family that settled in the former smithy at the end of our street. I was afraid to approach their old, dilapidated house, since I was warned by my playmates that Gypsies were evil. I was told they stole horses, ate exotic food, and brought bad luck. Worst of all, they kidnapped little children. My curiosity never quite allowed me to stay away. Once or twice, I managed to get close enough to their yard to catch a glimpse of the kids, and then run away as fast as I could. They were all dark-skinned and wore dark clothing. They also spoke a strange language.

What is fascinating to me now is the realization that as a child of Holocaust survivors, I could have also appeared "strange" to my Polish playmates. Fortunately, I did not feel like a stranger in my own country until I was much older. Language was never a problem. Polish, for all practical purposes, was my mother tongue. However, from very early on I was exposed to the conflicting worlds of hyphenated nationalities (Polish-Jew). On one hand, my parents tried, sometimes clumsily, to make me and my older brother conscious about their vanished world. On the other hand, I was sent to a Catholic nursery school. This nursery was run by nuns, whose mission was to make us all pious Christians. I was not familiar with any religious rituals and felt uneasy about kneeling and praying before meals. To this day, I am still unable to explain my parents' decision. It is possible that they were not aware that these practices were part of my nursery routines.

I learned the meaning of blind hate by discovering an album of photos documenting atrocities committed during the war, such as public hang-ings and street shootings in Polish ghettos. It was at this time that I began to sense that something terrible had occurred. My parents were not always sure how to share their life stories with us. It slowly became clear to me that our family of four was just a remnant of something much larger.

This view of a larger community was united in my mind over time with the "forbidden" language, which was Yiddish. When I say forbidden, I mean a language that was to be considered a death sentence not that long ago. While the war might have been over, postwar Poland was far from being healed of its hatred of Jews. During my entire childhood in Poland (I left Poland when I was about 14), Yiddish was never a language of pride. I would become particularly unhappy when my parents spoke it in the street, since I knew that Jewishness was publicly derided by adults and children alike. Children solve such problems by trying to blend in. We knew that if we wanted to stay out of trouble, whether in our own back yard, in the street, or in the schoolyard of the only school in Lodz that offered Yiddish, our Jewishness could not be flaunted publicly.

It took me many years before I was able to partake in the joys of Yiddish. The first instance occurred when I came across the English versions of classical Yiddish stories, such as Itzhak L. Peretz's *Bontsha The Silent* (*Bontshe Schweig*) and *If Not Higher* (*Ober Nisht Hecher*), and Sholem Aleichem's *The Pocketknife* (*Dos Messerl*). I found these translations to be mere shadows of the original stories I have read in Yiddish. I was particularly saddened to realize that I did not know many people who could share this knowledge with me.

In the late 1950s the Polish government decided to ease the immigration laws, and many Jews took this opportunity to leave. Though I knew throughout my growing years that I would eventually leave Poland, I was not emotionally prepared to do so. Like any teenager, I could hardly resist the promise of a great adventure. Yet I felt uncertain about the future, seeing everything we possessed parceled out and the rest squeezed into bundles and suitcases. Our newly acquired fabric-bound, dark blue passports that symbolized our freedom also stripped us of our fatherland. Our passports were marked CITIZENSHIP: UNDETERMINED. At the time I could not have foreseen that by departing Poland I would also forsake my closeness to the Polish language. It is a loss that I continue to mourn. Though I still speak Polish, time has irrevocably erased a particular sense of intimacy I shared with my native tongue, and the new languages I have since acquired, regardless of my efforts to "adopt" them, will never supplant the void created.

I did not question my parents' decision to leave Poland, the only place we knew, and with mixed emotions I followed them to the train that took us away. For days we traveled in packed cars, passing through Czechoslovakia and Austria to Italy. From there we eventually sailed for Israel.

I was almost 14 when I arrived in Israel with my newly acquired pony-tail and a bag full of youthful enthusiasm. The Italian ship *Pace*, which picked us up in Genoa and sailed with us across the Mediterranean, com-pleted its mission and now stood silently in the port of Haifa. We created some commotion. Unperturbed, the regal boat looked on indifferently as the few hundred Polish emigrants unloaded their lifelong belongings. Except for father, who decided at the last minute to stay behind in West-ern Europe, we'd made it to the land that had been promised to me ever since I could remember. My sixteen-year-old brother, Leon, was now the oldest man in the family. I entertained Marko, my four-year-old brother, and helped gather the array of valises, baskets, and bundles that had accompanied us on our journey.

Mom had to deal with the *Sochnut*, better known as the activists in white shirts and khaki shorts, who held our immediate fate in their hands. All the *olim hadashim* (newcomers) had their sights set on Tel Aviv, where we knew we would find more opportunities to get jobs and get settled. "Don't worry," they reassured her, half in Polish and half in Yiddish, "It's Tel Aviv . . . it's Tel Aviv." It took forever to get things organized and di-vide us up into groups. Finally we were loaded onto a caravan of buses, and the last leg of our journey began.

We were greeted in the *Yavne maabara* (a camp for newcomers) by a curious crowd. They were a lively bunch. As we got off the bus two young-sters approached us and attempted to explain something that we couldn't make out. Some women gestured, and mumbled strange-sounding words. *How odd*, I wondered, *that's what Hebrew sounds like?* The news spread very quickly that we were not in Tel Aviv, as promised by the activists, but more like 30 kilometers away, a significant distance there, and that most of our neighbors were Sephardic Jews. I was mesmerized. We were surrounded by golden sand dunes and people whose heads were crowned with *kaffiyehs* (fabric turbans). The men wore loose, white *sharwalls* (loose trousers) and pointy leather mules. Who knows? I pondered. They might have walked in the land of Ali Baba and actually touched Aladdin's lamp, and the brave ones could have sailed with Sinbad the sailor through the Arabian nights.

Among the hammering noises we were led by a *sochnut* representa-tive to our new home, which was being completed as we walked toward it. Laborers were installing doors and windows, and others painted the exterior walls. Our homes were really long concrete boxes divided by four doors, and each unit, or *shikun* (dwelling), belonged to one family. The *shikunim* (a row of connected dwellings) faced each other across the dirt road and gave the impression that they were just long trains, momentarily at rest, and would be taking off any minute. It was the whiteness of our freshly finished *shikun* that became for me the hopeful sign that things were as they should be. I lifted my head to face the new sky. It was cloudless and perfectly blue.

Mother had more mundane things on her mind. She was mainly concerned with feeding us. In no time she got in touch with people who guided us through the first days in the *maabara*. These were newcomers from Hungary, Rumania, and Czechoslovakia. What we shared with them was the language of Yiddish. They did not speak quite the same Yiddish, but different dialects of it. I noticed that proper names of vegetables, fruits, or dishes that seemed peculiar to their native lands became part of their Yiddish. So, for instance, corn was called *mamalyga* in Hungarian-Yiddish, and *kukurydze* in Polish-Yiddish. These were differences that were easily overcome. We bonded with the East European Jewry simply because we were all survivors of World War II, suddenly thrown together in a new land. We were also children who were educated in the Socialist model. The histories of our respective countries were taught to us from the same textbooks, and we all had to study Russian for many years. Though we did not speak Russian with equal fluency, we all laughed at the linguistic uniformity that the Soviet regime had imposed on us.

At sundown we would gather around our favorite spot, the front steps of our *shikun*. I still remember its smooth surface and the pleasure I had sitting there barefoot, my toes caressing the cool stone. Mom's face had changed. "As soon as I start working, we'll be all right," declared Mom with her newly acquired authority. At six o'clock each morning she was taken by a truck with twenty other newcomers to the nearby *moshav* (cooperative) to prune green vegetable beds and pick tomatoes. Slowly, I found myself in charge of our housekeeping. Marko was now my responsibility, and I had to learn to cook, while Leon was getting ready to go to the *ulpan* (Hebrew immersion course). Mom's philosophy was quite simple: "Leon must learn the language and acquire a trade. He's a man; he'll need to be a provider." "But Mom," I tried to object, "I'll have to do something. I can't stay home forever. You promised." She waved her hand impatiently, which was her usual way of reminding me that my gripes were pointless, and she proceeded to set me straight.

"You see, Fran, with you it's different. You'll get married and someone else will take care of you." Her tone left no room for any youthful rebellion. It all seemed so logical to her, I thought. To feed us was the first priority. Did I have the right to change the laws of nature?

As with youngsters anywhere, our Sephardic neighbors did not leave us alone for too long. They attempted to communicate with us any way they could. Our "Polish" conversations were now sprinkled with Arabic, Hebrew, French, and Italian. We were soon invited to the *Moatzei Shabat* (Saturday Night) dances in the local *moadon* (club). We listened to Elvis and

Paul Anka songs, without understanding a word of English, and had few difficulties dancing with a bunch of spirited youngsters who could not speak Polish.

Our new friends who came from Egypt, Morocco, Iraq, Syria, Yemen, Tunis, and Algeria might have been familiar with many languages, but they were mostly fluent in Arabic. With time I became so accustomed to hearing Arabic that I was able to distinguish a variety of Arabic dialects spoken by each nationality. I also befriended our next-door neighbors, the Cohens, an Egyptian family from Cairo: Mrs. Cohen, a widow with two grown sons, Solomon and Mousa, and a teenage daughter, Marcella. At first we just exchanged glances and smiled a lot. I was, however, too intrigued by Marcella's culture, customs, and food to remain silent for long. Shortly afterward we became so comfortable with each other that our language barriers begun to crumble. Since my French was rather weak, though it helped at first, I started picking up Egyptian Arabic. Slowly my Arabic became good enough to carry on simple conversations. Gradually, I was beginning to be known as the Polish girl who spoke Arabic. In order to communicate with my Hungarian friend, Julie, I picked up some Hungarian words, and with a small Hungarian vocabulary and some Russian thrown in, we "talked." Language did not seem to matter; we just tried to cope.

Though I did not know it at the time, I was partaking in a global village, where linguistic, cultural, and social differences were allowed to flourish. Hebrew, the official language of Israel, which eventually had minimized our differences and had the power to remake us into Israelis, was still months away.

5

From Bayamon to Brooklyn

RITA E. NEGRÓN MASLANEK

It was June 1954, a month before my sixth birthday. I remember boarding the plane in San Juan, Puerto Rico, with my mother and three-year-old sister, Lillian. I vividly recall the red-and-white homemade taffeta dresses Lily and I wore. Whenever I am in a fabric store, the unforgettable scent of the material instantly transports my thoughts to that warm summer night. Earlier that evening, my eight-year-old sister and seven-year-old brother gathered with my extended family in my grandparents' poor wood house to bid us farewell. We would soon be reunited with my father, who had left for New York a year earlier in search of the immigrant's dream. My siblings were to join us in three months. The excitement over our departure was almost overshadowed by the first lightbulb in *Mama's* house. *Papa*, my grandfather, stood guard on the porch where the bulb hung in naked radiance, making sure no one wasted light.

Within three months of our arrival in New York, my sister and brother joined us in our apartment in Brooklyn in a predominantly blue-collar Irish and Italian Catholic neighborhood. Assimilating was not easy at first, complicated by the fact that in addition to being non-English-speaking, we were also Protestant, which seemed to confuse almost everyone we met. "How could you be Puerto Rican and not be Catholic?" What do you mean, you don't know how to dance?" These were two questions I was to hear for many years to come, and often still do. Some of the kids on the block sometimes tormented us and often picked fights with my brother, perhaps because most of the tormenters were also boys. "You stupid *spic*," they would say. While I did not know what "spic" meant, tone and body language are universal. This definitely was not a friendly word.

"*Papí, que es spic?*" I asked. My father, who spoke a little English, replied that it was a derogatory term used by "gringos" to describe Puerto

Ricans. Dutifully, he proceeded to teach us to defend ourselves by calling these kids "stupid guinea" or "stupid mick."

My mother, who strongly disapproved of my father's teaching method, would certainly have been disappointed had she heard me exchange curses several years later with a fourth-grade classmate in a heated argument. Tired of being taunted, I armed myself with a grown-up curse I had heard my father use several times. "You sonamonbeech," I proudly yelled. "You what?" she asked. I repeated, "You sonamonbeech." Then the girl and a small crowd of spectators began to laugh at me. "You dumb spic, you mean *son of a bitch*," she said. It was then that I realized that the grown-up curse I had been saving for a special occasion was not one long word, but four separate words. I was humiliated, but felt more anger toward my father for his stupid pronunciation and the embarrassment it had caused me.

Aided by the acquisition of our first television set in the late 1950s, my English language journey continued uneventfully, for the most part. I discovered that the assimilation process included more than just learning a new language, it also meant learning about different foods, customs, and rituals. Christmas, for example, ended abruptly in this country on December 25, while in Puerto Rico the celebration continued through January 6, *El Dia de Los Reyes* (Three Kings' Day, or Epiphany), the day children generally received their gifts. And we quickly learned from neighbors' stares and comments that it was unacceptable to play in the rain, or more specifically, to stand under the gutter of the garage across the street from where we lived to let the summer rain cool our heated bodies. On the other hand, it was quite acceptable, and great fun, to play in the water pouring out of the *Johnny Pump*, or fire hydrant, as I was to learn years later it was really called.

Influenced by television shows like *The Donna Reed Show*, *Father Knows Best*, and *Leave It to Beaver*, I fantasized about a different life in green-covered lawns where mothers did housework in high-heeled pumps and strings of pearls, and where there was no fighting or arguing. Because most of the other families in our neighborhood were only slightly better off than us, our economic status did not separate us as much from our neighbors as did our nationality, language, food, and religion. Shouting and arguments overheard from open windows confirmed that in this department we also had some commonality. A religious-related ritual that at first made me feel excluded occurred every Wednesday afternoon in elementary school. At 2:00 P.M. all the Catholic children, which included most of the class, were dismissed early to attend religious instruction classes in church. I, however, received religious instruction during Sunday school at *La Primera Iglesia Bautista de Habla Española de Brooklyn*, a fundamentalist independent Baptist church where I was taught that smoking, drinking, and dancing were paths leading to eternal damnation and were strictly forbidden. The church became my refuge, the center of my social life, where I learned to read and write Spanish by way of the Bible. In this place everyone was like me—all Hispanics of the same faith and mostly recent immigrants. Ironically, as I got older and my world broadened, my religious identification often separated me as much from other Hispanics as it did from non-Hispanics.

In those days in public school, you knew who was in the "smart" class and who wasn't by the number that followed your grade. For instance, in the second grade the smartest kids were in classes 2-1 and 2-2. As this set of numbers ascended, the prevailing thought was that the level of intelligence of the children in these classes descended. If there were seven second-grade classes and you were relegated to class 2-7, you were an academic pariah, your destiny often mapped by this cruel classification system. While the system worked well for kids who were lucky enough to be labeled smart, others not so fortunate were marginalized, and this stigma often followed them to junior high school and beyond. I was one of the lucky ones.

These were pre-bilingual education days. It was English by immersion. Because I was a diligent student who loved to read, and perhaps because I was very young when I began to learn a new language, learning English did not prove to be traumatic. This is not to say that there were no difficult moments. One of a few early memories I have of my school days occurred in the second grade. We were learning the poem "Trees" by Joyce Kilmer. I was to read the line, "Poems are made by fools like me, but only God can make a tree." I did not know what "fool" meant, so I raised my hand and asked the teacher. For some reason unknown to me, my teacher scolded me without answering my question. Then all the kids broke out in laughter. I can still remember the public humiliation and sense of isolation I felt when I was trying so hard to fit in. That episode taught me not to ask questions when I did not understand a word. It also taught me that being funny was a ticket to being popular. Apparently the other children were not laughing at me, they laughed because I had made the teacher angry by asking her to define a "bad" word. To them I was a hero for being a smart aleck, and unlike my teacher, they believed this to be a positive characteristic. So I embarked on my new mission—to be accepted and liked by making others laugh. In this way, I thought, I could shed my "spicness," that part of me which separated me from the rest.

At the same time I was learning English, I was also learning Spanish. My father's Spanish-only rule at home was strictly enforced until the time came when it was just more natural and easier for my siblings and I to communicate with each other in English. There was also the added advantage that if we spoke fast enough we could actually speak about our parents in their presence without them catching on—well, almost never. Though we had abandoned the Spanish-only rule when speaking with each other, we always spoke in Spanish with our parents. To do otherwise was both unnatural and disrespectful.

Surpassing your parents in the dominant language of the place you live creates unusual circumstances. Often the children are called on to serve as their parents' interpreters. This was particularly fortunate for my older sister, Edna, who often translated for my mother more favorable comments about her progress in school than were being reported by her teachers. On many occasions I had to accompany my mother to one place or the other to serve as her translator. This early entry into the adult world influenced my behavior when I became a parent. Careful to shield my two children from a too rapid departure from their youth, I often did more for them than I should have.

Although English has been my dominant language for most of my life, I have always been more comfortable praying in Spanish, the language in which I learned to pray. Hymns sung in Spanish are more powerful and elicit more emotion from me than when sung in English. This strong identification with the language in which I was nurtured was even present during the birth of my first child. My obstetrician told me that although my married name is *Maslanek*, everyone in the delivery room knew I was Hispanic by the way I moaned. According to him, when "American" women moan, the sound made is "Ow, ow, ow," but Hispanic women in pain cry out, "*Ay, ay, ay.*"

When asked my thoughts on bilingual education, I must admit that I almost always disappoint the questioner, who is usually a proponent of this method of education. My response is informed by my personal experiences and by conversations with my siblings and other family members who came to the United States at the same age I did, or older, and who like me do not favor bilingual education. The only dissenting opinion in the group is that of one female cousin who arrived in New York at the same age I did. She is the only one among us who describes her educational experience as traumatic and claims she was scarred for life, an experience the rest of us do not share.

I am not entirely opposed to the concept of bilingual education. My cousin, who is a school guidance counselor in the New Haven, Connecticut, public school system, helped me to understand that the problem has been more to do with implementation and administration. I am painfully aware that many students who are products of bilingual education do not master either their native tongues or English at the adult levels. I have interviewed Hispanic job applicants, some who hold four-year college degrees, products of bilingual school education, whose English-language skills cannot be termed anything other than poor. Sadly, many also had poor Spanish-language skills. I blame a poorly planned bilingual education system for the failure to equip students with the proper tools to compete in a highly competitive society. While I believe that reasonable accommodations are critical to provide accessibility to otherwise prohibitive places or opportunities, the accommodations made in teaching English as a second language appear to be neither reasonable nor effective. It is unrealistic to expect any large urban school system to provide quality education in the multitude of languages represented by its immigrant student population. When poorly applied and administered, accommodations can result in greater limitations and obstacles than the barriers they are intended to overcome.

I have finished writing this chapter in Puerto Rico, where I came to spend Mother's Day with my now widowed mother. In many ways I feel as much a stranger here as I did during my first few years in New York. People who hear me speak for the first time quickly detect my "accent" (which I argue I do not have), that I am from *afuera*, the word used to describe those living in the United States. My errors, which they patiently correct, are often a source for their amusement. Adapting to the tropical heat reminds me of adapting to cold New York winters. The relaxed pace is in stark contrast to the rapid pace I have become accustomed to. As I reflect on my language-formation journey, I am reminded that for me, learning a new language was the easy part. Learning to fit in was/is the bigger challenge.

6

Writing for Effect

ELIZABETH NUÑEZ

In Trinidad we have this expression: "Mout open, 'tory jump out." When parents or teachers warn children, "Mout open, 'tory jump out" (mouth opens, story jumps out), they do not intend to merely send a cautionary message on the pitfalls of indiscretion. There are no metaphors to be deconstructed, no analogies to be sought. The words are meant to be taken literally: When you open your mouth to speak, the very words you use, your references, your tone of voice, above all, your diction and your accent reveal your life story. They tell of your economic and social status, your family background, your aspirations, your failures.

It was fear of this power of speech that made my father turn the slightest conversation with him into a battle, which we, his children, never won. "That's not 'd,'" he would insist. "Put the 'th' in that word. Take the 's' off the end of that verb. They do, not *'dey does.'*" As we struggled to inject "th"'s and "s"'s, our tongues snarled in that unfamiliar territory where my father wanted us to belong, and all color drained out of the tale that moments before had us squealing with excitement. Fitted into the strictures of the language my father demanded of us, our experiences suddenly sounded foolish, silly, unimportant, not worth telling. We were children of a colonized people, my father was reminding us. Any hope for our futures resided in our ability to mimic the colonizer, to speak his speech.

When ambitious middle-class parents in Trinidad feared their adolescent daughters were in danger of losing "th"'s irretrievably, they sent them to boarding school in England. One or two years were sufficient. These girls would return home with English accents, perhaps not at all authentic, but distinct enough from the one we used in Trinidad to make their story evident whenever they opened their mouths: they were not ordinary girls; they were middle-class girls. Boys got a reprieve. They could make their way in the world through education; good jobs awaited them. But a woman's future, until relatively recently, depended on the success of her mate. And she was more likely to be picked by a man with potential for success if the proper story came out of her mouth.

The working class, too, understood the social value of "proper" speech. By proper speech they meant speech that erased as much as possible Trinidadian syntactical structures and inflections, speech that did not seem to belong to a colonized people, speech that was spoken by people who did the colonizing, people with power.

There is this alienation, then, between language and identity that is established early in the life of the individual from a colonized or recently decolonized country. One is taught to develop false speech patterns, to separate story from the telling of story, indeed to understand that the telling has more value than the story itself. I think it is knowledge of this experience that motivated the celebrated novelist V. S. Naipaul to caution the writer Paul Theroux to avoid "misapplied words and meaningless mystification." In his book *Sir Vidia's Shadow* (1998), Theroux quotes Naipaul: "Don't use words for effect. Tell the truth" (p. 46). Earlier, Theroux recalls a time when Naipaul caustically dismissed the words "grommet" and "gusset" as silly, descriptive terms for the plastic covering on his car seat: "You see? But they are silly words. They are purely technical. There is no picture. They say nothing. Don't be that kind of writer. Promise me you won't use those words" (p. 26).

It is not clear to me from Theroux's narrative whether he understood the source of Naipaul's anxiety. He seems to locate it in the peculiarity of the man, and though no observant reader would be foolish enough to call Naipaul ordinary, in this instance his anxiety reflects an ordinary and understandable response to the commonplace experience of one whose early education occurred in a colonized country where the implicit message in composition classes was the importance of separating the story from the mouth, the story from identity, the story from the teller of the story, and, too often as a consequence, the story from the truth.

In my birthplace, Trinidad, where I lived until I was 18, where Naipaul lived until he was the same age, we were taught that make-believe has more importance than the reality; that our imaginative renderings of England were much more worthwhile than realistic portrayals of our tropical sun, our coconut tree-ringed sandy beaches, and our turquoise blue waters. Why else was I asked to write essays about snowflakes falling from the sky on a wintry day, about a host of golden daffodils dancing in the breeze, about picnics at the seaside with apples, pears, and peaches, none of which grew in Trinidad? Why else did not a single book I studied in high school tell the story of people who looked like me, nor was set in landscapes familiar to me?

By the time I graduated, I knew a lot about English history and litera-ture. I took pride in the fact that I could quote long passages from Chaucer, Shakespeare, Milton, Wordsworth, Keats, and a number of other English poets. I had read Fielding, Hardy, Austen, Brontë, and many of the other English novelists and essayists, yet I had no idea of the history of my own world. I did not know about the Amerindians, I did not know the history of slavery and indenture on my island. I knew that a few people who looked like me wrote books, but I understood that the books they wrote could not be important books, for if they were, my teachers would certainly have mentioned them. Of course, things have changed now with the indepen-dence of formerly colonized countries having occurred more than three decades ago, but habits die hard. Convictions cemented in the soul at a young age are difficult to eradicate, and adults, consciously or uncon-sciously, pass on this message to the young: your truth, your experience are not significant enough, not valuable enough to be put into print.

How could I write about mangoes when I was a child? Yes, I could certainly talk about mangoes. I could wax eloquently about mangoes (so long as my father was not monitoring my language); I could describe their texture, taste, and smell; but writing about mangoes felt strange, uncom-fortable. The paradox simply was that as a result of my elementary and high school education, when I eventually entered college I found it easier to write about something I had not experienced than to write about an experience I was familiar with. I could write about apples, but not about mangoes. To compensate for the insignificance of my world, I prettied up my experiences with lies, false words, and false sentence patterns. I wrote for effect.

A friend, a critic of my writing, complaining that my stories were all set in periods before I was born, urged me to write about my experiences: "You *tell* me such great stories," he said. I had tried. But how to write about that past in Trinidad? How to write about a life I had been taught was in-ferior to the life of the English child? When I was very young, I immersed myself in the novels of Enid Blyton about the adventures of siblings my age. I lived their lives in my imagination, but the world I returned to was not at all their world. My world was hot and sticky. Theirs was cool and shaded. They scampered across green meadows; I fought to disentangle myself from thick vines and snarling undergrowths. My world was black; theirs was blond.

I am pained each time I read the section of Jamaica Kincaid's *Annie John* (1983) where the eponymous main character longs for the world of Jane Eyre. It is the pain of recognition and embarrassment. In these times of political correctness, do I dare confess that I had this same longing? And yet my early writings reveal just that. The evidence is there in the way I decorated my experiences with flowery language, in the way I burdened them with tropes and weighty allusions and, yes, convoluted sentence structures that, unconsciously, I hoped would compensate for what I ultimately thought was material not worthy enough to be the stuff of written text. "Don't write for effect," Naipaul cautions. I could not write any other way and hold my head up.

Though indeed many of my teachers praised these early essays—my arcane vocabulary, my lush descriptions, my odd turns of phrase—I fortunately had the wisdom to know otherwise. Perhaps I sensed instinctively, in spite of the praise, that what I had written was a lie, and therefore bad. Good writing always tells the truth. My answer, then, to my good friend and critic who urged me to write about my reality is that I could not write about my experiences until I had confronted the lies about myself, until I discovered who I was. I know now that that discovery occurs in the process of writing itself. This is why writing is so satisfying, indeed therapeutic. (Even now, as I write this, I am making discoveries). Yet there has to be a willingness to confront one's truth before one sets off on this journey, a willingness to tear down barriers, not shore them up, if one hopes to accomplish writing that has value.

I began my first novel, *When Rocks Dance* (1986), with such willingness. I wanted to know what I really thought of my African roots. Of course, in the wake of the political independence of Trinidad from England, I spoke glowingly of Africa, and with confidence. It was fashionable to have pride in Africa, to speak positive words. But colonies survive because the colonist has managed to convince the colonized of the superiority of the Mother Country, that curious oxymoron. Andrew Salkey, in the introduction to his ground-breaking anthology, *Island Voices: Stories from the West Indies* (1965/1970), advises that in determining "how West Indian is West Indian writing," the critic "would be unwise to ignore the dominating influences of Western civilization, the long-term effects of British cultural and educational standards, the compelling attractiveness of English literature, and the use of English as *the* language in the West Indies" (p. 13).

In my heart of hearts, did I believe what I said about Africa? In an attempt to arrive at an honest answer, I decided on a dangerous route. I would write a novel that would juxtapose Obeah to Christianity. In the end, my sisters became so convinced of my conversion that they wondered whether I really did believe in what they called "that mumbo-jumbo." But conversion was not my objective. I had no interest in changing my religion. I did, however, make an important discovery that liberated me to write another novel, one that did in fact tell of my experiences. I discovered that for all the hoopla of 2,000 years, Christianity has no more monopoly on the way to truth and goodness than any other religion or philosophy. It was the arrogance of the Western world that made us think so.

It is from the perniciousness of this arrogance that I wish to free my students. At Medgar Evers College of the City University of New York, where I teach, roughly 80% of the students are first- or second-generation immigrants from former British colonies in the Caribbean. Many are also from African countries with similar political histories. This is the problem I confront as a teacher of writing: My students do not trust their voices. They believe that their speaking voice is for *telling* the truth, their writing voice for *inventing* the truth. The result, of course, is that their written expressions are forced and false, their sentence structures and word patterns so convoluted that often neither they nor I can decipher any coherent meaning. What does this say? I ask. They have no answer. Why did you write it, then? They are silent. And I hear Naipaul's plea to Theroux: "Promise me you won't use those words." Later, "Don't use words for effect" (p. 26). I beg my students: Promise me you won't write those kinds of sentences. Promise me you will listen to your voice. A colleague complained that for the life of him, he could not get his students to commit themselves to a thesis statement that reflected their own views. I understand. It is problem I struggled with for years as a young girl.

Now I want to shake the cobwebs out of my students' heads. I want them to affirm the value of their beliefs, visions, and realities. I am willing to do anything: be a buffoon with my silly jokes, spread my life before them, let my skeletons out of my closets, anything that would help them see the absurdity and danger of falsehood, false words, false sentences. I want to help them (and me, too) find the courage to write their truths, to claim the English language as their own. "You taught me language; and my profit on't/Is, I know how to curse," says Caliban to Prospero, the man who would be his master (*The Tempest*, 1.ii.363). I tell my students: The language is yours. Bend it, twist it, curse if you must, if doing so will take you to the point of familiarity, of ease, where the written language becomes your vehicle, too, your conduit to the expression of your reality. Do it for your own sake. Do it for the world's sake.

My father has advanced in age. I refuse to say he is old. All his gray cells are intact, perhaps frayed at the edges, but in better condition than most intelligent men half his age. Now the man who pounced on all the "d"'s I used to supplant the "th"'s in the conversations I had with him, who insisted on "s"'s at the end of singular verbs in the present tense even though doing so changed my stories dramatically, many times stripping them of their original meaning, has dropped his "th"'s, replaced them with "d"'s, and is unconcerned whether his verbs match his nouns, or, for that matter, whether any of the inflectional endings of his words are "proper" or not. "De yout today," he says, alarming my son, who was straitjacketed by me to speak "proper" English in front of his elders, "dey never lissen."

I make a joke of it. I ask him, as in the game *Wheel of Fortune*, whether he wants to buy a "th" from me. He laughs. He is comfortable with himself. After years of camouflaging identity for the sake of giving evidence of his intelligence, his worth, he is in the castle of his skin. He is his own judge. *He* validates himself. And now he tells me true stories—about his past, about the humiliations he suffered, about his triumphs.

I am not making a case here for the use of idiom, dialect, or conversational speech patterns in formal writing. I appreciate the value of conventions. Conventions give the speaker or writer access to an audience. In informal situations, too, conventions serve this essential purpose. Certain ways of phrasing, terminology, and expressions convey specific meaning for specific groups. Outside of these conventions, meaning often gets distorted. But I want my students to have access to more than a local audience. I want them to communicate with the world. So I teach them the standard conventions of grammar and composition, but I do so for the sole purpose of empowering them.

For too long, for too many people of color, communication with the rest of the world has been a one-way street. I want the conversation between my students and the world to be a dialogue, a two-way discussion. I judge my success as a teacher of writing by my students' ability to speak their minds, to write what is in their hearts and thoughts in such an effective way that they cannot be ignored, that they transform even the reluctant, that they become equal participants on the world's stage in the ongoing dialogue for progress.

References

Kincaid. J. (1983). *Annie John*. New York: Farrar Straus Giroux.

Nunez, E. (1986). *When rocks dance*. New York: Putnam.

Salkey, A. (Ed.). (1970). *Island voices: Stories from the West Indies*. New York: Liveright. (Original work published 1965)

Theroux, P. (1998). *Sir Vidia's shadow*. Boston: Houghton Mifflin.

7

Learning to Speak:
One Woman's Journey

RUBY SPROTT

My identity as a child growing up in Harlem in the 1940s and later in a predominantly white neighborhood in Queens was forged out of a mix of linguistic influences: my natural efforts to speak to my peers in the street language that they spoke to me, to speak to my parents the way they demanded I speak, and to speak in school in a manner that was a little of both. I sometimes wondered if this was the way for everyone. I didn't think so. It seemed to me that some people could speak one way all of the time. There was no ambiguity in their speech habits. As an adult I learned that, yes, others did have these same conflicting influences in their lives. I was not unique. We black people do wear a mask, and code-switching, that is, changing back and forth from the vernacular to Standard English, is a living reality that emerges out of a desire to remain sane and to stay alive.

My early childhood in Harlem was an exciting initiation into the language and customs of the streets. I remember playing near our stoop almost every day. Our speech was thick with *ain't*s and double negatives as we played jump rope (double dutch was my personal favorite), hopscotch, and ring-aleevio-Coca-Cola 123. On cold nights older boys would light a fire in a barrel and roast sweet potatoes. Everybody on the block knew each other, and we all, especially our parents, knew where on the block they could go to play numbers. Ring-aleevio-Coca-Cola was a noisy game. Someone would call out in a loud voice, "Ring-aleevio-Coca-Cola 1-2-3," and the crowd of children would scream and scatter with someone running after us. I still don't know what those words meant, but every syllable filled us kids with the joy of unadulterated street play. Much of our game-playing involved raucous, animated screeching. Quiet games or cerebral games were not in our game repertoire. There were no word games or games involving higher-level thinking skills out in the street, but the games we did play were full of touching and moving and talking and screaming and inventing new rules. We loved our lives in the street. We didn't have to watch our language, and there was constant laughter. Even if we knew there was another way to talk at home or at school, in the street we were completely free to say what came naturally.

At home it was a different matter. My mother was acutely aware of the Black collective struggle, and she was afraid for her children to be a part of the world without mastering Standard English. So at home even more so than in school in those days, my mother would constantly correct us. There was no corruption of grammar in our house! No matter what we were saying or where, at the dinner table, in the bath, anywhere, she would call out to us, "Say it right!" Her voice was strong, emphatic, unsympathetic, and relentless. I never questioned how she knew what was right and what was wrong, but she did indeed.

At times she would even remind us to "speak right" as we left the house. She always said that she wanted us to be able to get a job. That was her aim. Just "speak right" and get a job when you graduated high school. She feared that without the language of the dominant culture, we would join the legions of others and herself who cleaned rich people's houses.

In spite of my mother's limited education, she was an avid reader. There was always a crossword puzzle in the house, and we had family games that I'm sure unbeknownst to her reinforced our love of language. We'd spend hours at family gatherings, perfecting our individual and partner strategies playing card games. From the age of about 10, words like "bid," "hearts," "spades," "clubs," "diamonds," "trump," and a host of others became a part of my living vocabulary. Language was an essential part of these games. In addition to the puzzles and card games, my mother instilled the love of reading as she read to us. She read us fairy tales and scary stories. Those stories where boogey men came to the foot of the bed and tickled toes and the ghosts lurked on the dark streets of St. Eustatius (the small island in the Netherland Antilles where my parents were born) scared me silly, but established for me and my sisters a firm foundation in literacy and a love of learning.

Muh, as I called my mother, also took us places that steeped us in a diversity of rich sounds, smells, and social influences that were intertwined with my language acquisition. As we held onto her coat, she regularly tramped us over to the Park Avenue Market, the area under the "el" train where she could buy fresh fruit and other vegetables, as well as fish and meats. I would wonder where the el went and would imagine myself traveling from coast to coast, stopping along the way to explore the Grand

Canyon and to discover if there was salt in Salt Lake City. The Market was a part of El Barrio and was a place where the sights and sounds could overwhelm you. My mother would walk through the market very fast, with us practically running to keep up with her, until she came to a section where she wanted to buy something. I may have blocked the sounds of *Español* at the time, but later, it must have been because of those sounds that I wanted to study Spanish in junior high school. I loved the sound of phrases like *muchas gracias* and *por favor*.

It wasn't just my mother who played an important role in my empowerment through language. It was the genuine attention to my attempts to use language by Black teachers such as Mrs. Harris and Miss Gooding that made the difference. They demanded our best work, and they got it. I don't recall any child in my third and sixth grade classes who could not skillfully handle written text. We read in school. We talked in school. We performed and played in school. As bell hooks (1984) would agree, it was the language of the oppressor that I was learning, but it was giving me a tool to share my thoughts and emotions. I didn't know it then, but I, too, was working hard to master the language that would give me the tools to later succeed in college and graduate school.

Yet I wonder if I didn't lose something valuable when I lost the language of the street: the warm, democratic language of my childhood friends. What I really lost was the spontaneity of language that they had. They didn't seem to have to worry about code-switching at home, and at school they got by. Those days in Harlem on the street, in school, and in my home gave me a sense of the possibility of empowerment that would not die, but I do regret the way I sometimes felt as a child about my ability to "talk well." I was always commended by teachers, and when people met me after talking with me over the telephone, they were always surprised that I was Black. In the days of my childhood and young adulthood, before I was politicized, those compliments filled me with self-assurance and pride. How sad!

One incident that made me regret the loss of street language occurred when I was about 11. There was a small candy store around the corner from the apartment building in Harlem where my parents were the superintendents. I could buy penny candies, pickles from the pickle jar, and sticks of bubble gum. Once the storekeeper even let me go behind the counter and pretend I was the shopkeeper. I was very naive and impressionable then. I thought he was the kindest man until he squeezed me where he shouldn't, and for a long time I was terrorized and stopped buying those goodies that I loved so much. Did I use my facility with English to tell my mother and father? No! I knew that he had done something very wrong, but yet I felt less like the victim and more like the guilty one. Maybe if I could have told him in the language he understood best (street language or expletives) what he had done to me, I would have felt some relief, but even then the language of the street was fading from my memory. My mother's insistence on standard speech and all I had learned in school had begun to inhibit my ability to get to the nitty gritty. That would have been the best language (both profane and unmentionable) to free my soul from the insult to my body. In spite of my loss of the vernacular language of my early childhood in the streets of Harlem, I learned that my life was full of the sweet, the exciting, the intriguing, and the sometimes terror-filled. We moved from Harlem when I was 12, and it was then that my richly filled days and nights came to a resounding halt. We moved to Jamaica, Queens, where we'd be the second Black family on the block.

My life changed dramatically with the move to Queens. In and out of school there was an emptiness of experiences worth remembering, and this also affected my linguistic development. We no longer had a stoop outside our house where we could sit and play. We no longer had the games and camaraderie of the other kids on the block, and we no longer had the candy store with penny candy and other goodies. But most of all, my experiences in school were different. School was unaffirming, sometimes hostile, and most of all not the rich learning environment of my school in Harlem. At P.S. 24 in Harlem, I had been a top student. I loved school because the teachers cared about us. They taught us about Harlem, about the city, and the nation. They took us on field trips and invited inspiring speakers for us. I will never forget the time when Helen Keller visited our school in Harlem and spoke to us in her different-sounding voice about her life, her lust for knowledge, and her love of learning. I remember recitations in the assembly and the praise I would receive about my work.

All of these empowering school experiences that had nurtured me came to a stop in Queens. For a while I was silenced. That silence manifested itself in apathy and lack of academic productivity on my part. I simply existed in the class. I was not really a part of the class. My language skills did not develop much more, due to the apathy that manifested itself in literacy game-playing. Yes, I had mastered the language of my mother's dreams and of the school, but this language was without imagination and color. Instead of reading everything I should have, I read Cliffs notes, blurbs and conclusions and used my literate imagination to expound upon plots, characters, and influences. Since my teachers didn't value my voice, it didn't matter to me. The students in Queens were not my friends the way I had friends in Harlem, and I often felt ignored. From the ninth grade on, I was the only African American child in most of my classes.

Even though I was silenced for a while, language remained in my head, heart, and soul, and I eventually found other opportunities to develop my voice. There was one other Black student, Dorothy, in some of my classes. She lived not too far from me, and she became my very good friend. We both used the church as our vehicle of empowerment. It was in the church that we could act in plays, recite poetry, and participate in discussions that were meaningful about social issues. And it was in the church's young people's groups that whatever voice we had developed could be affirmed. Without the church, our sense of ourselves may have died. In school, even though we did well academically, we did not participate in extracurricular activities, and we never really felt as if we were a part of the class or the school. I didn't participate in class discussion, and teachers didn't seem to care.

The one exception was the modern language teacher. After two years of Spanish, I decided to try French. That French teacher was the only memorable teacher of my high school years. Maybe it was the nature of a modern language, which demands that the teacher listen to you, advise you, and really hear you. During that year of French, our teacher planned a class visit to a French restaurant and a French film. We had real experiences that year that affirmed everyone, especially me. At last I felt some connection in that school. I could use my language, even if it was not English.

I often look back on those days and wonder how I managed to continue my education after high school and to believe in myself. I attribute all of my strength as a student to my formative years in Harlem. It was there that I became a literate being and learned that I had a voice worth listening to. Since those few short years in Harlem, I have not seen either of my most memorable teachers, Mrs. Harris or Miss Gooding, but I often think of them and the strength of the teacher to empower students and to also make learning real. For a few short years, I was affirmed as a special person who had something valuable to contribute. Those few short years made a world of difference for me, and today, as a teacher, I know that my students also need many affirming experiences—experiences that help them to know who they are and how they fit into the world picture. Perhaps, even at the college level, I can help them to become literate by listening to them and giving them power to be whoever they are. That has been my life's work.

Reference

hooks, b. (1984). *From margin to center*. Boston: South End Press.

8

Identity Conflicts and Literacy Development in First and Second Languages

RAIMUNDO MORA

I was born in Quito, Ecuador's capital. However, my father, who wanted me to be Colombian like him, hid the fact that I had been born in Ecuador, and smuggled me into his country, where he obtained a birth certificate saying I had been born in Colombia. Then he took me back to Ecuador, where six years later, I started elementary school. After finishing third grade in Ecuador, I was taken to Santuario, a rural town in the Colombian Andes, where I started fourth grade and faced the first identity conflict I can remember. My conflict started when I unsuccessfully tried to speak and behave like my Colombian classmates, but I could not help acting Ecuadorian.

My classmates found it hilarious that I called my sister *mi nañita* (the word for *sister* used only in Ecuador) instead of *mi hermana* (the standard word for sister). They mocked me till I could not take it anymore and got involved in fistfights, which earned me some respect. The other kids stopped picking on me, which was quite a relief. However, they also stopped talking to me, which meant isolation. Since I was left with no friends, I became an eager reader. My main entertainment was to go to the movies to watch Mexican films, the only ones shown in the local theater, and to read whatever I found at home. There were no libraries or any other source of reading materials in town. I did not like to read textbooks. They reminded me of my painful isolation in school. At home, I first tried to read my father's books on medicine, but since I could not understand them and the pictures of deceased and dissected bodies disgusted me, I chose to read my mother's romance novels. I related to them instantly since they reflected the love songs, boleros, and tangos that my parents used to listen to all the time. I was also interested in the radio soap operas that my mother used to listen to. It was through these soap operas that I became acquainted with my first English literary piece. It was a translation into Spanish of *Wuthering Heights* by Emily Brontë. The orphan Heathcliff became my hero. Like him, I wanted to leave town and come back rich. Reading romance novels and listening to soap operas prepared me for writing love letters. I started by writing love letters to fictitious girlfriends in which I recreated the romance world I had discovered through my reading. I showed them to my classmates. My reputation as a good love letter writer grew to the point that students from other grades started commissioning letters. Through literacy I gained some acceptance among my classmates.

My career as a letter writer was interrupted when I finished my elementary education and was sent to a boarding school in Pereira, a small city near Santuario. In the boarding school, I did not find ways of reading and writing that motivated me to read and write in the ways the soap operas and love letters had done. My literacy practices were reduced to reading textbooks and writing reports with endless lists of names of places, events, and authors that frequently did not mean anything to me. In the literature courses, for example, I was given a textbook that contained brief autobiographies of authors and equally short descriptions of their work. I never was given pieces of literature to read, which might have perked my interest in the same way that romance novels did. I began reading classical literature when, by the time I was in 10th grade, an uncle who lived in Bogotá, Colombia's capital, started inviting me to spend holidays with him. He was a self-educated journalist who lived in a farm near the city. When I visited him, he used to set up my bedroom in his library, where he kept a large and eclectic collection of books. There I read diverse books such as *Don Quixote* (parts of it), *La Celestina*, and Spanish translations of *Exodus*, *Lolita*, and *Lady Chatterly's Lover*.

In the boarding school, there were many students who like me lived in the school facilities. There were other students who lived with their families in Pereira. Those living in Pereira came to school only during the day. From the beginning, I felt like an insider in the community of resident students. During my four years in Santuario, I had to learn to speak and behave like them. Like them, I had gone to Pereira from a small town. We presented a united front to protect ourselves from the attacks of the students who did not live in the school and who considered themselves superior to us because they were from the city. However, I don't remember feeling inferior, probably because we outnumbered the city students. This rivalry was particularly apparent in class performances. We, the resident students, helped each other academically, making sure that we did not fall behind our rivals. When I graduated from high school, I was heartbroken to leave the school. This was the school I felt I belonged to. Afterwards, for many years, I had recurrent dreams in which I went back to a secure and happy life in that boarding school.

Since the idea of going back to Santuario was far from attractive, I decided to attend college in Bogotá, where I lived with my uncle for a short period of time. Then I moved to the student dorms, where I experienced my second major identity conflict. I had to learn from scratch how to speak and behave so that I was accepted in the college environment. The new game was not to sound provincial. I had to learn about classical music, literature, and theater. I learned the social rules of my new environment by listening very carefully to people. I learned that with fish I was supposed to order white wine and that I should never mention having become acquainted with *Wuthering Heights* by listening to soap operas. Instead, I learned to speak about the literary value of Emily Brontë's novels. Since the weather in Bogotá was cold compared to that of the area where I had grown up, I had to learn to dress warm. I also had to dress in a European style. Fashion was an important social marker in this city. There were lots of jokes about the way people from hot climates dressed in Bogotá. I tried hard. I was intrinsically motivated. I was seduced by the sophistication of the city. I wanted to be part of it.

During the first academic year, I met a group of students from Bogotá and we just clicked. We became inseparable until we graduated four years later. They introduced me to social circles in Bogotá in which I could test how well I had learned the social and cultural codes of the upper classes in Bogotá while I was in school. These friends and my social life became the most important part of my life. While in college, I do not remember having been interested in the courses I took. I just did what was necessary to pass the courses. I discovered that I had a special ability for statistics when I started getting excellent grades with a minimal effort. On the other hand, I had serious problems with written assignments. Since I kept a distance from the content of the courses, I could not get too involved with business-related topics. To avoid writing, I used fancy statistics that required little written explanations.

After earning my bachelor's degree in business, I worked for the Colombian government in a program involving industrial development. Several years later, I faced another identity crisis because I could not stand my job any longer. Actually, business never held any interest for me. I chose it under the influence of my father, who thought I needed a lucrative career. This realization came strongly when I started getting a lot of satisfaction from teaching swimming as a volunteer in the Red Cross. This satisfaction awakened in me my earlier desire to become a teacher, so I decided to make a radical change. I left the country to start anew as a teacher in the United States.

I moved to New York, where I went through another acculturation process. It involved adapting to Spanish-speaking and English-speaking communities. In New York, I stayed with an uncle who lived in Corona, a Hispanic working-class neighborhood in Queens. This uncle was one of my mother's brothers who had moved from Ecuador to the United States 15 years prior to my arrival. He lived with his wife, two sons, and a daughter. His other children, one son and three daughters, had married and lived nearby. My uncle, his sons, and his sons-in-law worked in the construction industry and in factories. His wife took care of the house, and his daughters and daughters-in-law worked in supermarkets and also in factories. Everybody was close to each other. They had meals together at my uncle's house, watched baseball games on TV, and had parties on the weekends. They communicated in Spanish among themselves. They spoke and behaved according to Ecuadorian norms, the same ones I had learned growing up in Ecuador. However, during the time I had lived in Colombia, I had become different from my Ecuadorian relatives. During the six months I lived with them, I experienced difficulties acclimating to their culture. I remember feeling defensive about adopting their identities because I did not want an identity imposed on me, like the one I had left behind. I felt that the communities I wanted to identify with were somewhere else, so I started to look for them.

The section of Corona where my uncle and his family lived was predominantly Hispanic. Next to it, there was another section of Corona that was predominantly African American. I decided to explore this section in order to find opportunities to practice my English. However, the attempts I made to break the ice with Blacks were a failure. I do not know if they were a failure because my English was limited or because they did not want to break an unspoken rule that African Americans and Hispanics did not mix, at least in this neighborhood at that particular time.

Since I needed to learn English in order to attend graduate school, I realized that I had to move from Corona to an environment where I could interact with English-speaking people. By that time, I had studied English as a foreign language at the high school and college levels in Colombia. I could understand some written English but I could not communicate orally, probably because I had been taught English through the grammar-translation approach. I enrolled in an English as a Second Language program at LaGuardia Community College. I started at the second ESL level and it took me two terms to exit the fourth and final level. One year after my arrival in the United States, I moved to Manhattan. By this time I had finished my ESL courses at LaGuardia and started graduate school at New York University. Since I had saved some money in Colombia, I could enroll as a full-time student in the Teaching and Learning Department. From all the options that the department offered in education I chose the Teaching of English to Speakers of Other Languages (TESOL) Program. The logic behind this decision was that my experience learning English as a second language was going to inform my studies about how people taught and learned a second language.

I was admitted to the graduate program under the condition that I took ESL classes simultaneously with graduate courses. From the beginning I found the graduate courses helpful for both my teaching education and English acquisition. The fact that I wanted to be well prepared for my new teaching profession highly motivated me to work hard to be able to understand what my teachers and classmates said, as well as to comprehend the written materials I was asked to read. In contrast, I experienced intellectual alienation in the ESL classes. I remember my despair attending some ESL classes because their content was banal compared to the content of the graduate courses I was taking. In one of the ESL courses, the teacher asked students to read children's books, arguing that we were not prepared to read adult books. Also, I remember having to do endless exercises of controlled writing, which did not lead to any meaningful writing. What led me to meaningful writing were the graduate courses' written assignments on language learning. Although I had serious language limitations in regard to my English, the subject highly motivated me. This motivation led me to create a writing community with classmates, friends, writing tutors, and an occasional professor who helped me prepare and edit my papers.

Improving my oral skills was another matter. Nobody seemed to know how to help me. My phonetics teachers gave up trying to have me hear and produce certain sounds in English. At the end of this course I received the only "C" I got in school. Meanwhile, I could not participate in the discussions of the other classes. Each time I had something to say, it took me forever in my mind to prepare the language I needed to express what I wanted to say, so by the time I was ready to speak, the moment to say it had already passed.

With classmates and particularly with professors, I frequently had communication conflicts and breakdowns. I used to blame my linguistic proficiency without realizing that there was a body of sociocultural knowledge that I did not have and that I needed to gain in order to use effectively the linguistic knowledge I had. For example, on one occasion, I was having a difficult time finishing a paper that was due for an appointment with a professor, so I decided to break the appointment with the professor, an older lady, in order to finish the paper. I ran over to her office, told her that I could not make it, and left with no further explanations. The next day, I had a class with the professor and gave her the paper I had written for her. To my surprise, she took it disdainfully, without saying one word. She had been the only professor who had shown interest in helping me with my English difficulties. I was upset with what I perceived to be an act of rejection. She did not pay any attention to me for the rest of the semester. Years later when I, already a college professor, ran into her in a conference, she confided to me that when I had canceled the appointment with no explanation, she concluded that I had very bad manners and did not take my studies seriously. Retroactively, I understood that at the moment I entered the professor's office I had not found the right words I needed to express what I wanted to say, so I had resorted to an informal simple utterance. I thought that my casualness matched the professor's informal way of conducting her classes and talking to me. In Colombia, I would never have opted for a casual tone with professors, since they were very formal in the way they dressed and conducted their interactions with students. When I started college in the United States I was shocked to see professors wearing blue jeans and sitting on desks while lecturing their students. Probably it was then that I started to get the wrong idea that teacher casualness equaled student casualness.

By trial and error, I learned that to communicate effectively anywhere involves not just learning grammar and vocabulary but specific norms of language use. The communicative competence model has helped me understand conflicts that originated from the rejection of English speakers because they found my behavior inappropriate. For example, when I used a casual expression to cancel my appointment with a professor, I used an inappropriate register. Had I been taught polite expressions in English to apologize, I might not have resorted to casualness. Had I been aware of the formal register students use when talking to professors, I might have elected to expose my linguistic limitations rather than act casual.

My teachers also used language inappropriately with me in some of the ESL classes I took. For example, when one of my ESL teachers had me read children's books, I felt patronized, trapped in a surreal world. Fortunately, I received a lot of satisfaction being treated as a teacher in the graduate courses. Otherwise, I think, I would have dropped out.

Being treated as a teacher in graduate school helped me assume a teacher identity that put me in a position to express myself as a professional. In this position, I brought together the persona that had been shaped in Colombia and the one I was shaping in the United States. Even after completing doctoral studies and working as an educator for many years in the United States, the challenge continues to not allow my academic discourse in English to overpower my identity in Spanish.

Part II

MOTHER TONGUES

One obvious reason for learning the language spoken by one's parents or grandparents is to enable a person to connect more strongly to the family and its history. There is also the more politically charged motivation of reclaiming or giving voice to a silenced language. What happens when children grow up speaking a language different from their parents? Some may internalize the dominant perspective that their native languages are superior to their parents' "minority" languages. Those who can relate to their parents' experiences as outsiders may be more likely to connect with them by speaking their languages. In validating what the larger society considers "lower-prestige" languages, they challenge the status quo.

The tenacity of longing and desire to reclaim identities that the dominant culture attempted to wipe out is felt strongly in Pramila Venkateswaran's piece, in which she describes the costs of her privileged education in India, an education that produced high levels of literacy in English at the expense of her native Tamil. After immigrating to the United States and earning a Ph.D. in English literature there, she eventually returns to her early attempts at reading and writing in Tamil and discovers that learning her mother tongue not only brings her closer to her mother and India, but also to feminist values inherent in Tamil language, literature, and culture, which she had not found in English.

Fredy Amilcar Roncalla also views his language and cultural experiences through the lens of colonialism in his reflections on relearning his native Quechua, which he was forced to replace with Spanish as a young child. Written via postmodern, scholarly, and political writing, he uncovers the irony of identifying more closely with Andean culture after being transplanted from Peru to the United States. The physical distance provides a greater space for him to explore his Indian roots and become more aware of the role of hegemony in shaping self-perception and identity.

Mimi Bluestone describes studying Yiddish as a process of "tapping into a genuine linguistic residue within (her)self" in order to pass onto her children a language she once abandoned. In taking on the arduous task of regaining a lost mother tongue, she found something she perceived had been lost in her 20th-century life.

Susan Driscoll's journey to connect with her mother's native language and culture brought her to Korea, where she gave voice to the Korean part of herself that was silenced while growing up as a biracial child in the United States. Strong themes of dislocation emerge in her piece as she reflects on how both cultures objectified and even mistreated her for being somewhat different.

Paralleling Driscoll's description of the impact of racism, the next two writers in this section discuss the immense frustration and sense of invisibility they have faced by being visual communicators in a dominant auditory-language society. These two essays provide a fascinating dialogue as the two writers approach the topic from different standpoints in relation to Deaf culture. Susan Stocker, a native speaker of English, describes her painstaking process of assimilating into the mainstream rather than living in a Deaf subculture, which she accomplished through extensive training in lip reading and linguistic pronunciation. Through helping others to accommodate her, such as by looking at her when speaking, she was able to fully integrate herself into a hearing world. Margie English, on the other hand, was born into a family of American Sign Language communicators. Her piece allows us to hear a strong voice affirming Deaf culture and provides insight into the picturesque world of sign language.

9

Language, Exile, and Discovery

PRAMILA VENKATESWARAN

It is a typical evening in Bombay. Pink skies creep across the fringes of the city. From our balcony on the third floor I can hear and see the rush of traffic up and down the highway. Below me, children have gathered in the building compound and have begun yet another game of I-Spy. *"Niche ao"* (come down), a voice travels up toward me, beckoning me to run downstairs. "Face wash *pannitu po,*" advises my mother, propelling me toward the sink, mixing Tamil and English with hardly a thought that they are different languages. Below, among the rush and tumble of the city, children play games with English names, sing English rhymes, "Ring a ring of roses" and "Oranges and Lemons," but speak to each other in Hindi or Marathi.

My experience in Bombay nearly 35 years ago is still true today. I now live in the United States, a transition in my life that has made me even more aware than in previous years of my attitude to language learning. We have lived in the Northeast, mostly on Long Island, for 16 years. During this time, I have been studying, teaching, mothering, and writing, all activities that have often placed me in groups where I was the only person who spoke a language in addition to English. In the predominantly white suburban community I live in, bilingualism is something one reads about in the newspapers; a foreign language is something a family thinks about when their kid has to decide on a choice of language in junior high. My children, my husband, and I equate "American" with being a monolingual, only-English speaker. Even the term *bilingualism* is often understood as Spanish and English, since the closest neighbor to the United States is Mexico and also since Mexicans and Latinos are noticeable, although only grudgingly acknowledged, in the history of the United States. A universe of languages abounds in every street corner, restaurant, subway, and university in this country, but these languages are not given a nod of recognition, due to the predominance of English.

People in the United States are usually amazed when I tell them I am multilingual. They think I must have a rare talent for languages, but I quickly inform them that my particular cultural context shaped my language learning: I was born in Bombay, a region where the predominant language is Marathi; Hindi is also spoken widely, a phenomenon common in most regions in North, East, and West India, other than Uttar Pradesh, where it is the dominant language. Since my parents were Tamilians from Tamil Nadu, in South India, we spoke Tamil at home. My mother's schoolbook knowledge of Hindi helped her adapt to Bombay, and she continued to improve her Hindi speaking skills. During my childhood years in Bombay, I learned to speak Hindi from friends who spoke the language at home and used it as the main medium of communication in their games in the apartment compound. When I was four, my parents sent me to an English-medium school, where the instruction, the script, the nursery rhymes, and the books were in English. Contrary to some people's belief in the United States that a child gets confused if taught more than one language, many children, like me, grew up in Bombay learning two, three, and even four languages.

However, looking back I can honestly say I was not an experienced or well-honed speaker and writer in Tamil and Hindi, since my thinking and writing were shaped in English. As an adult I constantly felt that I was monolingual rather than bi- or multilingual. Often I even felt illiterate and balked at friends, family, and the government who pointed their fingers at the illiterate peasant as a problem in society. Knowing English, I felt, divorced me not only from the illiterate people around me but also from the people educated in the regional languages who spoke expressively about issues and ideas I felt disconnected from.

As the years of schooling shaped me, English became my primary language, used as a mode of communication about all professional, educational, and even emotional matters. I used my mother tongue Tamil less often in my interactions, even at home. My brothers, my sister, and I communicated mostly in English, and sometimes in a mixture of English and Tamil, a phenomenon quite common among children being educated in English. My love for English literature grew at 12 when we were introduced to Shakespeare's plays in school. In high school my skills at English essay writing improved, and I continued to work at achieving nuances of expression, which I failed to achieve in Hindi, which was my second language in school.

When I was 11, we moved to Calcutta. My father's job as a manager in a nationalized bank led to him being transferred to a new city every three to five years. In Calcutta I had to study Bengali, a mandatory language in school there. I also had to study Sanskrit and Hindi. Some of this burden lightened the following year in seventh grade, when Bengali was no longer required, but Hindi and Sanskrit still were. Moreover, my mother felt I needed to have at least a rudimentary knowledge of Tamil, and sent me to a school where Tamil was taught on Sunday mornings. I didn't find learning my mother tongue to be much work, but drew the alphabets as if they were icons of art, and pretty soon mastered the 200 or so letters. But reading Tamil was a challenge. It took me an eternity to read a sentence.

At 15, I did not get beyond reading jokes written in Tamil in magazines. Reading Tamil fiction, I felt, needed patience that I did not possess. Moreover, English took all my attention, since I was majoring in liberal arts in high school and had decided to major in English literature in college. My fluency in English led me to embrace it even further. But I did not inquire into why I was studying English literature as opposed to Indian literature written in any of the regional languages. It was only years later, while studying for my M.A., that I began wondering about my lack of reading and writing ability in Tamil. I realized I was out of touch with my own country's emotions and ideas expressed in its literature, and out of touch with my mother, whose education and personal growth was located in Tamil language and literature.

Over the years she had read me stories and poems in Tamil, and I had absorbed all the characters and sayings, songs, and ideas. Kannagi's lament in *Cilappatikaram* at her separation from her husband, then her forceful argument in the king's court indicting the king himself for his lack of justice in wrongfully seizing and killing her husband, resonated in my mind through my adolescence. Avaiyar, the Tamil poet-saint, sang in my mother's voice into my ears that loved poetry. Comic detectives like Tupparian Champu, very much like the Pink Panther, also entered our Sunday afternoons in Madras, when my mother read to us the detective's stumbling methods of unraveling mysteries.

In college, I acutely felt that my English education was in the way of my finding the importance and the time to devote my attention to learning Tamil. I felt this all the more when a course called Indian Literature was introduced in the English department at Bombay University the year I graduated with a master's degree. I remember being excited that Indian literature had finally made its way into the English curriculum, but felt a sense of loss at discovering that Indian literature only included texts written in English, not the regional literatures, which collectively shared a rich history. The English department in India was after all a reflection of society and history. My betrayal of my mother tongue was a natural outcome of more than 200 years of British colonial rule: English had displaced

Indian languages, and westernization had displaced my sense of an Indian self.

Indian writers like R. Parthasarathy (1976) speak of the exile of the Indian reflected in his exile from his mother tongue. In "Homecoming," he uses the metaphor of the chain to picture the oppression of the colonized in having to use the oppressor's tongue and describes his desire for the mother tongue as an unassuaged hunger.

I experienced my exile with pain. I did not fit into my country. I did not fit into my family. I felt I was being educated to live away and apart from my parents and what they had known. During these years I felt my exile as a woman for the first time. In rejecting the oppressiveness of society's attitude toward women with systems like dowry, lack of choice in marriage, and so on, I felt, the opposite pole, or safe haven, was westernization, which in my imagination stood for freedom. My paradoxical situation was that I felt "liberated" as a speaker of English, but without its rewards in the form of choices to me as a woman: I was reminded with each of my experiences that I was an Indian woman, modern because English opened up paths for me, but at the same time exiled me from family and society because of my education.

When I was a student in the Ph.D. program in the United States, I wrote letters to my mother in English, which, I thought, was absurd. My natural expression with my mother should have been in Tamil. But English enabled me to use multitudinous modes of expressing my emotions that I had not been educated to express in Tamil. At the same time, writing in English opened up a gulf between me and mother. As the years sped by, filled with comprehensive exams, proposal writing, and dissertation research, my heart ached to close that widening gap in my relationship, separated by history, language difference, and geography. I wrote in one of my letters to mother, "Do you remember, you used to tell me stories by Sivasankari? Can you send me some writing by her?" In a few days, I received a novel by Sivasankari called *Ini* ("Hereafter"). The Tamil letters looked like a mass of interesting sea creatures floating across the pages. I focused all my energy and read the first paragraph: The words rushed into me and out, some of them making sense, some of the words sounding like nonsense, but I was persistent. If that paragraph did not make sense, I told myself, the next one would. Within a few hours I finished the first chapter, and I was exhausted. Reading Tamil was like reading a foreign language. I was tasting the juices of an alien tongue, and for the first time I was getting into its sensibility. I did not want to give up. For the next few days I sat with that book. The progress was slow and painful, with missed meanings, confusion, and triumphs, but I got through the novel. As I progressed from chapter to chapter, the reading became easier. Finally, I was through. I had gotten not merely the text but the subtext of the novel, and I was inquiring into the writer's imagination and her intention in the novel.

Since then, each time I pick up a Tamil book to read, I feel intimidated, but once I doggedly follow the rows of characters that lead to the periods at the end, I become more and more triumphant that I am entering a world that was foreign to me until now.

When I visited my mother in India after I had finished reading my first Tamil novel, I could discuss it with her in Tamil. She shared more of what she had read. Reading Tamil built a new bridge between us, and since then she sends me some of the feminist writing in Tamil that is making new landmarks in Tamil fiction, stories that deal with women meeting challenges, circumventing circumstances, questioning chance, and persisting in recreating themselves despite the onslaught of society and history. In my exile I had felt that only knowledge of English could open up avenues of freedom for women. But in delving into the Tamil stories I had heard in my youth and in the fiction I am now reading, I am finding women who are passionate, forceful, empowered, and imaginative, showing me paths within my history and culture that colonialism and English education had kept away from me. I am also discovering that the characters that spoke through my mother reading to us from Tamil literature had left their traces on me as I was growing up, shaping my mind and helping me direct my life.

Entering India through Tamil, I discover the rage, passion, and possibilities of freedom expressed by characters and writers in Tamil fiction. Freedom does not live on party lines, East or West. It is a deeply felt need in every human being, and each of us expresses it and has a right to it.

Reference

Parthasarathy, R. (1976). "Homecoming." In R. Parthasarathy (Ed.), *Ten twentieth century Indian poets*. Delhi: Oxford University Press.

10

Fragments for a Story of Forgetting and Remembrance

FREDY AMILCAR RONCALLA

I.

I was born in Chalhuanca, a small provincial capital in the Peruvian Andes. My family was mestizo (people of Indian and European descent). My mother's side descended from a generation of impoverished land-owners, and my father came from faraway Arequipa as a coca and wool merchant. By virtue of my mother's family, I was supposed to belong to the local elite in a society where the mestizos were at the top and the indigenous population at the bottom. That meant that I had to be raised in Spanish, not Quechua (the main Peruvian Indian language). As a prestige language, Spanish was mandatory for the mestizo kids, who were, for the most part, prohibited from learning Quechua. The stigma of "Indianness," much stronger in the 1950s than now, had to be avoided.

Quechua was spoken everywhere. Not all the mestizos could afford to stay in town on a permanent basis, and from the very beginning my mother had to work in a small village, Totora, which was one day by truck and another by horse or on foot away from Chalhuanca. She was a school-teacher. She taught Spanish in the midst of a Quechua milieu. Meanwhile, I came in close contact with the indigenous population. I learned my basic Quechua.

Ever since those early trips from Chalhuanca to Totora, I have been moving from place to place and language to language. Traveling has been my home away from home. By the time I came back to Chalhuanca I was able to witness how the mestizo kids made fun of the indigenous students and those who came from rural areas. They also made fun of me since I had lived in the Indian *puna*, or high-altitude plateau. I knew early on that the dominant groups use sarcasm and humor to discriminate and degrade anyone who doesn't speak the same language they do, in this case, colonial Andean Spanish.

One morning my parents gave me a package. We opened it carefully and there was perhaps the most important gift I have ever received: a book. It cast a huge spell that has since led me to buy thousands of titles and carry them all over the continent. I also recall the beautiful music of the people singing from the heart that talked about love, loneliness, traveling, leaving home, and thinking of coming back. The mestizo songs would switch between Spanish and Quechua and the Indian songs would be mostly in Quechua. Those songs have been my protective mantras in all my travels, and they still are the place where my inner contact with Quechua is strongest.

II.

When the Spaniards showed up out of nowhere, the Incas had established Quechua as a lingua franca in the Andes, where many other indigenous languages were spoken. The trauma of the conquest introduced Spanish and writing to the Andes. (There was no writing in the Andes, although Quechua is not only a spoken language.) The Spanish quickly occupied center stage in the Andean linguistic interplay, but those times were also good for the expansion of Quechua. Both the church and the colonizers needed an instrument to gather information, to control and to indoctrinate the indigenous population. So, very early the priests, who were the first anthropologists and linguists, began writing dictionaries, grammars, catechisms, songbooks, and sermons in Quechua, while the colonial administrators relied on their translators to carry out their destructive task.

At the end of the 17th century, Quechua was well established in the Andes at the expense of many regional indigenous languages. Quechua was a cohesive factor in the Tupac Amaru Indian rebellion that started in south Cusco and expanded in other areas, mainly around Lake Titicaca, where Aymara is the other main Indian language. The Tupac Amaru rebellion was a threat not only against the Spanish crown, but also against the early *criollo* nationalist class, composed of descendants of the Spaniards born in Peru, who were claiming more rights to the country than the Spanish and the Indians. The rebellion was brutally repressed and eventually defeated.

After Tupac Amaru's defeat, the speaking of Quechua was officially banned. With this event the long colonial process of linguistic and cultural domination was put into place, and perhaps this is where we have to look when we want to trace the history of the shame that accompanies speaking an indigenous language in Peru. In this period, about one-quarter of the native population was wiped out. The Eurocentric ideology of the 19th-century criollo nationalism led to the perception of the Indian as a threat, as backward, and throughout the continent massacre after massacre was carried out in the name of the dubious contradiction between civilization and barbarism.

In the early 19th century the criollo successfully struggled for independence from the Spanish crown without the participation of the indigenous population at large. Shortly after independence, a massive expansion of the haciendas over communal lands began and the indigenous communities were forced to embark in endless legal maneuvering in an alien tongue: Spanish.

To see how the criollo ideology, now placed at center stage and evolving around Lima, would treat not only the Indian but also the Andean Spanish speaker as a source of scorn, one would have to go deeper into the events of the 19th century. One important incident concerns the insults made between 1836 and 1839 by a minor criollo poet from Lima, Felipe Pardo y Aliaga, against Marshal Andres de Santa Cruz, who wanted to create a Peruvian Bolivian confederacy, but carried the unforgettable sin of being from the Andes.

One of the main ways in which coastal Spanish speakers mock Andean Spanish is by pointing out the influence that Quechua syntax and phonology have on the regional Spanish. They also deride the fact that most Andean speakers cannot distinguish the between [e] and [I] and [o] and [u], because Quechua has only three vocalic phonemes. Poor Pardo used this fact to paint Santa Cruz and all Andeans as stupid, archaic, and ignorant, but he never realized that the joke was on him. The scorn about the vocalic sounds is based on ignorance of phonetic laws, and the false pride of speaking Spanish and thinking of it as a mark of superiority.

Thus, the tragedy of the criollo spirit becomes apparent: You hate what is yours and make it marginal and inferior (Indian) while you admire what oppresses you and makes you want to become "the other" (European). This deep contradiction and estrangement of the colonial spirit is readily apparent in the language of sarcasm, but has much more brutal consequences in times of social conflict.

A lot of the scorn used in the 19th century was transported into this century and led to an internalization of the linguistic discrimination and cultural and political domination. While the discriminators used scorn, the discriminated internalized shame. This is the background that the Andean and provincial migrants had to deal with coming into the coastal cities, mainly Lima, from the 1940s all the way to the 1990s. For the Quechua speaker as well as for the Andean mestizo, the arrival would mean a concealment of the mother tongue (Quechua) or the regional norm (Andean Spanish) in order to fit into the popular criollo speech of the city. And we see yet another paradox of linguistic oppression and colonial spirit: You acquire the speech of the one who scorns you in order to hide your own speech and make fun of the one who reminds you of it.

III.

By the time I made it to college I had already started writing some poems and thinking of myself as a bohemian. I had also spent a few years reading a bunch of encyclopedias, fantastic tales, newspapers, political pamphlets, and so forth. So I considered myself ready to further my studies at the Catholic University of Peru, alma mater to the great majority of the Peruvian business, political, and cultural elite. On the first day of classes, being an Andean migrant who had managed to acquire the lower-middle-class criollo speech of Lima in order to function, I was amazed to be around the kids from the upper classes, those you could only see in TV and magazine photographs, or read about in the papers. But not even the wildest premonition would have prepared me for what was to come. As I sat in the General Linguistics class I could hear the words in Spanish, but could not understand anything my teacher said. The words I had read and spoken all my life suddenly made no sense and I sat the hour, day, week, century that the class took to end feeling totally lost and ignorant. I had been exposed to the language of the elite without being ready for it. The words were the same, but there was a certain order in the syntax and a certain use of meaning that I could not relate to. From this very moment I was aware of the tremendous differences of class and prestige in Peruvian Spanish. I also understood, intuitively, that I could not fit into this system and eventually had to leave it.

I remember that during the months after the initial trauma of college I devoted myself to making up for the linguistic gap and spent most of my time in the library. I also spent a lot of time in the streets and cafes of downtown Lima getting involved with the young artistic movements. I immersed myself in many subjects. I understood little, mistrusted a lot, but kept trying. Perhaps I had not overcome the shame of my first day of class and had to come back with a sense of revenge, asking obtuse and baroque questions of my teachers, or writing papers that nobody could possibly understand. Perhaps the exclusion of the Andean culture was so intense in the curricula and the speech of the professors that I had a lot of trouble recognizing my Andean self. I managed to have the "honor" of getting the lowest grade in the philosophy class, because I had chosen to do a paper about Kierkegaard and I could not see how, if Kierkegaard was right in his critique of Hegelian reason, you could write anything using the same reason. Something similar happened the next year with good old Descartes, whom I felt was cheating because in order to say he doubts everything and then jump into the existence of God and the prevalence of reason he had to rely in a previously known logic, most likely of the Aristotelian kind.

I managed to bring out a certain nastiness in a few of my philosophy professors, which reminded me of my high school English teacher trying to mock me in front of my classmates for being a *serrano*, a derogatory term for somebody from the Andes. In the meantime I was becoming involved with underground poetical movements, subscribing to the idea that poetry comes from the streets, and that the task of the avant-garde was to go to the limits of language and change the world.

I also decided to pay more attention to my Quechua. In those times it was very difficult to find anybody who spoke Quechua openly. I had little desire to seek the people from my town, whom I considered a bunch of mestizos I did not want to associate with. The solution was to find whatever written material was available in Quechua and start learning to read it. Thus, I began not only to relearn Quechua, but to be exposed to various regional dialects.

IV.

A few years later, a lot of my intellectual and personal life evolved around Quechua. At the same time I was learning English, I had been hired as a Quechua–Spanish translator by an anthropologist studying Andean culture. I worked both in the Andes and in the United States.

During the first weeks in the Andes I had to relearn my Quechua, because I was in the Ayacucho area. My Apurimac dialect was different. I also had to prove I was an Andean because nobody believed such a tall guy could speak Quechua. Apart from the general goal of the research, my own interest was personal: a deep reconnection with my Andean self and with the culture, landscape, people, and music that I had been longing for.

After conducting field work in Ayacucho I spent two years in upstate New York transcribing and translating the materials we had collected. In the United States I forgot all the English I had studied in high school. Sometimes I answered in Quechua when talking on the phone. But I was able to start translating a few months later. I explored the bohemian and counterculture scene of Ithaca, New York. Also, I immersed myself in both avant-

garde social and cultural theory and the Andean anthropological literature in Cornell's libraries.

Once back in Peru I applied for a job as an English teacher, but got
one as a Quechua teacher instead. A lot of my students were history and
social science majors. I was able to combine teaching of Quechua with the
discussion of Andean culture. I began to be known as an anthropologist
even though I had not finished my studies in linguistics and had never
studied anthropology in a formal way. I also did some sporadic translation work from Quechua to Spanish and from English to Spanish. Translations were the bridges between my different homes. One of the jobs I got
was with a peculiar Japanese anthropologist who came to Peru to write a
book on the theory of chaos and marginality and left without leaving a trace.
He would dictate in broken Spanish and English and I would put the manuscript together in Spanish. We finished a manuscript that was never edited
or published. I learned a lot with him, but it took me a long time to distinguish between the creative aspects of chaos and the artistic fear hidden
behind my bohemian life.

Little by little I could see myself becoming an anthropologist, but I had
not resolved my artistic and creative aspirations. I began feeling torn apart
by the diverse cultures and languages I had been exposed to. It was then
that I got more and more involved with the bohemian life of Lima and
became increasingly estranged from the university. Finally, in the early
1980s, I dropped out completely, and left Peru in a state of creative silence.

After moving to Vermont, where the New England accent sounded
totally alien to me, I was able to solve some of those contradictions by
writing my first book of poetry, *Canto de Pájaro o Invocación a la Palabra* (Singing of the Bird), and putting a song in Quechua as the core metaphor among
a series of surrealistic and free-form verses. One of the underlying meanings of this poem is a search for a poetic voice capable of responding and
overcoming the poetics of death and power that I perceived to be all around
me. I do not know if this poem and my other writings have succeeded in
this task, but it seemed that the issue of language, power, and violence was
an important one, given the fact that the Peruvian Andes were in state of
civil war.

V.

The reflection on the language of death, politics, power, culture, and
representation concerning the war between the Peruvian establishment and
the guerrillas is only one of the many aspects of this painful time in Peruvian history. But it is necessary to point out the toll of this war on the

indigenous people, Andean, and Quechua speaking population. The people from the Andes and the native populations of the jungle were the cannon fodder. There were countless massacres against the indigenous population carried out both by the Shining Path, a Maoist guerilla group, and the government. The tongue of the indigenous became the language of the suspect—of the body that was endlessly mutilated and did not even deserve a proper name in the mass media. The government was busy naming their own dead, and defending the boundaries of their version of society and reality. The language of the Shining Path became equally official and oppressive, abstract, and deathly. Language fed and represented violence in a recurrent ritualization of death, with the indigenous as the choice scapegoat. Entire regions were forced to leave home and migrate—once again—to the greater cities and abroad.

The radiance of death gave the indigenous an ambiguous presence in the national scene. The stories and songs of the victims were being heard as the war moved to urban spaces. Suddenly the music from Ayacucho took over the national acoustic landscape. Academics and others increasingly felt the need to understand the Andes in a new way. While some voices predicted the disappearance of Andean culture, others talked about the birth of a utopia.

Migration proved the cultural permeability of Andean people. Once engaged in the criollo culture in order to survive, the Andean populations ensured continuity by means of reciprocity and festivals. The festivals were privileged spaces where the use of Quechua would enable you to connect with home. Some voices started speaking in first person from an indigenous point of view, and began the long task of overcoming the shame of speaking in public with an indigenous voice and language.

Another consequence of the war and the implementation of neoliberal economic terrorism in the 1990s is the huge flow of migration *from* Peru. Many people from different walks of life have left Peru, and live all over the world. For the indigenous and Andean population this constitutes a second migration. For those immigrating to the U.S., English becomes a third language to deal with. Suddenly Spanish is the discriminated language, and "Hispanics" the embodiment of the "other." Meanwhile, due to recent interest in multiculturalism in the United States, and to a romantic vision of the spiritual value of the decimated populations, the indigenous body and language are the choice presence in the field of vision of the academic, and popular, mainstream. Many people who came here thinking themselves western or criollo are being called Indian and forced in a different direction in terms of identity. It is as if the spell of the criollo culture of Peru was confronting its limits, and people were free to explore their own heritage and identity, memory, and shame. This landscape has allowed the Quechua language and culture to emerge on a popular level. There are many instances of people being more exposed to Andean music in the United States than in Peru. Also, the interest in the Andes can be seen in countless Quechua web pages and e-mail names in the Internet.

For their part, many Peruvian Andean academics and intellectual migrants working in the United States are beginning to explore questions of Andean culture and continuity. They're producing a vast and diverse literature. Even though I left academia a long time ago, it is there that I find my point of insertion as an Andean artist and intellectual, working in a postmodern multilinguistic space, and using the three languages I was given to express myself.

11

Memory and *Mameloshn*:
Learning Yiddish Then and Now

MIMI BLUESTONE

Like white hair and wrinkled skin, speaking Yiddish was part of old age. Or so I thought as a child. Yiddish was the *mameloshn* (mother tongue) of my grandparents.

But by the time I was born, even my grandparents were calling on Yiddish only when English lacked the power to say what must be said. With my grandparents carrying on most of the business of life in English, my parents never learned to carry on a whole conversation in Yiddish. No one in my home read a Yiddish newspaper or turned on the Yiddish radio. Instead, Yiddish haunted my parents' English, a ghost that made itself heard in a rising and falling of the voice, a few choice phrases, a handful of words.

But not just any words, words that scorch and wither, tickle and taunt. Why would my father call someone a jerk or a bastard when he could call the guy a *schmuck* or a *mamzer*? For my grandmother, saying "stop making such a fuss" couldn't compare with telling me to "stop making such a *tzimes*," a rich, fruity stew. "Don't bother me" paled beside *"hak mir nisht keyn tshaynik,"* quit banging on my tea kettle.

English was the invisible air we breathed, the transparent water we drank. Even in minute quantities, Yiddish was true substance, the language that cut through to essential meanings and relationships, the language for piercing pretense and lancing behavior not worthy of a *mentsh* (a decent human being).

There were so many reasons my grandparents' generation chose to leave Yiddish out of their children's inheritance. The Jewish immigrants of the late 19th and early 20th century have been called a "one-generation proletariat," and in the case of my grandparents, the move up from the sweatshop was even faster than that. The labor of a few sacrificial family members paved the way to middle-class American life not only for my parents but for my grandparents. English was an essential *lingua franca* of that life.

The diluted Yiddish of my childhood should have disappeared by now. But while she was still in high school, my mother began traveling a route that eventually brought me back. Determined to be as "American" as possible, my mother's was among the first Jewish families that moved to Riverdale, then an upper-middle-class neighborhood at the far edge of the Bronx. But my mother took a left turn in the 1930s, influenced by girls like her high school friend Lillian, whose father was a member of the Communist-dominated furriers' union. In the early 1950s, while I was taking in the Bronx from my baby carriage, my mother ran for the New York City Council and New York State Assembly on the American Labor Party ticket.

Later, in the suburbs just north of the Bronx, my atheist mother sent her children to the Sholem Aleichem Folkshul, a secular Jewish school. In *folkshul* we learned Yiddish instead of Hebrew. In place of religion, we studied Jewish history and culture served with a generous helping of left-wing politics.

Unlike the official environment of public school, *shule* was *heymish* (homey), its teachers and teachings informed by social and political passion. We called the teachers by their first names, learned Biblical stories, sang Yiddish songs, danced, celebrated holidays, and argued about ethics.

The Yiddish language got short shrift—a glossary of essential terms, a handful of verbs, hardly any conversation. Nouns hung alone in the air, unsupported by verbs and isolated from idioms. By fifth and sixth grade, my French teacher had covered reflexives, and I could tell time or ask about the weather. But I didn't have a clue that Yiddish also used reflexives, and everyday subjects like time and weather were somehow too mundane to cover. More important were words that conveyed essential information about a vanishing world, words like *khokham* (sage), *shame* (synagogue caretaker), *mishpokhe* (family), *melamed* (teacher of young children), *shnorer* (beggar), *makheteyneste* (my child's mother-in-law), *shlemiel* (a clumsy fool), *mitzveh* (commandment or good deed), and *mekhaye* (a real pleasure).

The effort to teach us to read was even more haphazard. My struggle to decode *alefbayz* (the Hebrew alphabet) made reading *Motele un Gitele geyen in shul* even less interesting than reading *Alice and Jerry Go to School*. It was wishful thinking to believe that in less that an hour a week children would learn to read texts in a language they didn't speak and printed in an alphabet they barely recognized.

Besides, there was so much else to do in the three hours we spent each week in *shule*. There was Yiddish literature in translation, with stories about boys drafted into the czar's army for 25 years, a magician who brought a Passover feast to a starving couple, daughters who defied parents and matchmakers, and a rabbi who celebrated Yom Kippur by disguising himself as a peasant and chopping wood for a sick widow.

There were songs, some with haunting minor melodies, others with rousing revolutionary fervor. In first grade, they were simple: *Bulbes* (Potatoes), *Tumbalalayka* (Play, Balalaika), and *Friling iz Do* (Spring is Here). The *shule*'s community Passover seder was a high point of the year, with special songs to learn: *Shvimt dos kestl oxfn teykh*, about baby Moses floating in his basket, and *In Dem Land Fun Piramidn*, about hard labor under Pharaoh. As we grew older, we learned Holocaust resistance songs: *Shtil Di Nakht*, about a girl who blows up a Nazi truck, and *Zog Nit Keyn Mol*, the Partisan hymn.

In 1973, when I was 20, knowing some Yiddish songs and how to accompany them on the guitar landed me my first full-time job. I worked in the recreation department of a senior residence and nursing home in the Bronx run by the Workmen's Circle, a Jewish fraternal organization.

Mamele (little mama), the residents called me. Unlike my upwardly mobile grandparents, these immigrant men and women had never relegated Yiddish to memory's attic. *Mameloshn* was their preferred language of conversation, the *shprakh* (language) of dining room announcements and the home's closed-circuit television station. Every resident received a daily copy of *Der Forverts* (*The Forward*), a newspaper. I would sit and read it with tiny, white-haired Lena. Her beautiful blue eyes could hardly see, but she would help me sound out the headlines: "Vah-ter-gate, Nik-sun, Vah-shing-ton, Kiss-in-dzher."

My collection of Yiddish words was too limited for conversation—in fact, I don't think it even occurred to me to try. The residents seemed to enjoy having me lead singing in Yiddish, but they must have considered my repertoire limited. I learned some of their favorite songs: *Sheyn Vi di Levone* (Beautiful as the Moon); *Fisherlid* (Fisherman's Song), about the fish and the lover who got away; and *Ikh For a Heym* (I'm Going Home), with verses in Yiddish and English: "I know that I'll be joined by at least a million more, Tel Aviv, we're coming, open up the door!"

My understanding of these Yiddish songs was usually based on available printed translations. I learned new vocabulary but made no systematic effort to understand the whole. Entire structural elements whizzed right past me, unnoticed. I didn't really care, thinking I could sing the songs intelligently enough.

After a year, I went back to college full-time. Yiddish wasn't on my agenda. American history was, and Spanish seemed more relevant than Yiddish. But I missed singing Yiddish songs. For Passover I would photocopy song sheets and pass them around to friends and family. But people who hadn't grown up with these songs didn't share my feeling for them. I tucked Yiddish away in a private, lonely corner of my psyche—until, at the very end of 1994, I went to Klezkamp and found myself, for the first time in 20 years, immersed in Yiddish culture.

Klezkamp is a week-long Yiddish folk arts program. Held each year at a hotel in the old Borsht Belt of the Catskill Mountains in New York, Klezkamp grew out of the revival of eastern European *klezmer* music, the dance music played at Jewish weddings. Traditionally, *klezmer* was instrumental music, but the klezmer revival has swept Yiddish songs along with it, and Klezkamp has become a place where you can sing in Yiddish from morning till night. Beyond music, there are workshops in literature, history, theater, film, calligraphy, and the eastern European art of paper cutting. Many participants know barely any Yiddish, but some have spoken it all their lives. Others have claimed Yiddish as adults and now speak it fluently and even teach others.

This "Yiddish Brigadoon" that comes to life every December soothed my *benkshaft* (longing). But there was something else. Those Yiddish songs—songs whose sounds and syllables were permanently engraved on my memory— were filled with words, idioms, structures, and meanings that I understood only in a distant, general way. The language and the songs stirred something deep, almost primal within me. But there was a simultaneous unfamiliarity that was jarring. I should be able to understand these songs, these words, the conversations taking place around me. Why couldn't I?

A workshop on translated Yiddish literature of women jarred me further. In the last decade, I discovered, dedicated translators had made Yiddish stories and poems written by women available in English. *Found Treasures* (Forman et al., 1994), an anthology of women's stories, was hot off the press, and it was the source of much of the reading in Irena Klepfisz's Klezkamp literature workshop. This was a new world for me: I couldn't recall reading a single piece of writing by a woman in *shule*. These stories by women had a stark, lonely quality that set them apart from the work of the best-known Yiddish writers, Sholem Aleichem, I. L. Peretz, and Mendele Mocher-Sforim. The Klezkamp song repertoire was another new world. In my sleep, I could sing *Friling Iz Do* (Spring Is Here). But I didn't even know the word for *autumn* until I heard *Harbst Lid* (Autumn Song), Beyle Schaecter-Gottesman's bittersweet meditation on autumn and aging. There were songs rooted squarely in religion, something new for me. Both *shule* and the Workmen's Circle home were secular places where it was pretty unlikely that you'd hear anything like *Hamavdil Beyn Koydesh Lekhol, a* song about the ceremony ending the Sabbath and the dread of facing another week of work and want. In my childhood, and at the Workmen's Circle home, songs about poverty tended to be humorous, but the Klezkamp repertoire encompassed more somber songs of deprivation—songs that we as North American Jews could now afford to acknowledge.

"Redn a Yidish vort iz a guter shpas"—To say a Yiddish word is a good joke, complains Beyle Schaechter-Gottesman (1990, p. 52) in her poem *"Mir Hobn a Gute Zakh"* ("We Have a Good Thing"). Yes, that had been my experience. Now I was moved by the beauty of Yiddish art songs, the sophistication of Yiddish poets who wrote with *eydlkeyt*, refinement.

Suddenly it seemed that mine had been a child's-eye view of *Yiddishkeyt*, one that saw the whole world of Yiddish culture encompassed in a few songs about holidays and resistance. I felt an overwhelming need to "grow up" in this culture, to fill in the gaps between my childhood knowledge and my adult self.

Back in New York I found myself reading obsessively about the history and culture of Yiddish-speaking Jews. And I discovered a Yiddish class offered in a small *shule* five minutes from my home, on the only night of the week that I would not need a babysitter to attend. It seemed *bashert* (fate) that I should go. *Mazl* (luck) was with me too: the teacher, Shulamis Dion, was a wonderful guide who brought passion, clarity, and creativity to her classes.

As the weeks went by, the songs that were a part of me became a valuable resource, one that I could mine for associations and contexts. When Shulamis introduced the uses of the word *tsi*, a word used at the beginning of a statement to mean "whether" or "if," I had an immediate association: the words, committed long ago to memory, of *Shtil di Nakht*, one of the songs I learned in *shule: "Tsi gedenkstu vi ikh hob dikh gelernt, haltn a shpayer in di hent?"* (Do you remember how I taught you to hold a gun in your hand?) Trying to remember whether *forn* (to travel) uses *hobn* (*to* have) or *zayn* (to be) in the past tense, the words to the lullaby *Rozhinkes mit Mandlen* (Raisins with Almonds) came swimming out of memory: *"Dos tsigele iz geforn handlen,"* the little goat went to market.

Shulamis provided the solutions to all sorts of puzzles. For example, why was a song about a grandfather's tune called *Dem Zeydn's Nign* when the word for grandfather was *zeyde* and the male article was *der*? I had had no idea that there was a whole case system of articles and noun endings. This news was not entirely welcome: It seemed that Yiddish grammar required lots of concentration.

Shulamis also cleared up some mysteries of the written word. I needed only a little review to bring back the letters, but it became clear that none of my previous teachers had ever fully explained their uses. For example, *alef* (a) is used silently at the beginning of words that actually begin with other vowels—a vital piece of information I don't remember ever hearing before. Soon I was able to sound out virtually all Yiddish words v-e-r-y s-l-o-w-l-y in a process that made me much more sympathetic to my seven-year-old son's struggle to read English.

But there was a catch to my blossoming literacy. I had never understood before why certain words could stop me cold in the middle of a sentence. The reason was actually pretty simple: those words were Hebrew. Yiddish is largely Germanic in vocabulary and structure, with Slavic elements and a sprinkling of words from Romance languages. But Yiddish is also full of words that are Hebrew, or Hebrew-Aramaic, or that build a Germanic form around a Hebrew root. Although all of Yiddish is written in the Hebrew alphabet, the phonetics used for words of European origin are quite different from the phonetics that apply to Hebrew words.

A useful discovery, but again, a sobering one: If I really wanted to read literature in Yiddish, I'd at least have to learn something about those mysterious Hebrew phonetics. And I'd need to fill in some of the gaps in my secular education, which had not prepared me for the complexities of the deeper Hebrew subtext undergirding vocabulary, idioms, and content. "For every folk story there was a Biblical legend, equally immediate but with far greater historical resonance," wrote Irving Howe (1976, p. 223) in *World of Our Fathers*, his monumental history of Eastern European immigrants in the United States. "For every folk song there was a cantorial melody tied to rituals of worship. For every folk witticism there was a passage of rabbinical commentary, speaking for the obligation to make moral distinctions."

Even while discovering new depths to my ignorance, I could still feel some satisfaction in at least knowing why certain words had me stymied. And I felt a great sense of accomplishment in learning to crack the general code of *alef-beyz* in both its printed and script forms. Writing Yiddish script became a compulsive activity, something I did consciously with pen and paper and unconsciously with my fingers while waiting for buses, riding on trains, and sitting in boring meetings.

And Shulamis kept providing new rewards for learning to read *alef-beyz*: song lyrics, poems, and a hilarious series of original dialogues set in contemporary New York. Health clubs, Indian restaurants, fire escape gardening—Shulamis's dialogues met contemporary New York head-on in Yiddish. I will never forget the Yiddish word for *stairs* because of one of

her characters, who tells his sister she needs to spend more time on the
trepmayster.

Yet the more I learn, the more overwhelmed l become with the depth
of commitment, the depth of knowledge required to learn a language and
its idioms—and to learn this language in particular, with its tangled roots
and branches.

There are times when I become discouraged and wonder why I want
to learn Yiddish at all when most of its contemporary speakers are extremely
Orthodox Jews with whom I have virtually nothing in common. Or why it
is that I want to spend so much time rummaging in the remains of what
poet Jacob Glatstein called "an abandoned culture" (quoted in Howe, 1976,
p. 452). Abandoned, yes, and murdered, and silenced.

But I already know the answers, and one of them is love: love for the
songs, for the sounds, for the thoughts that can only be expressed in this
particular way. Another answer is that learning Yiddish helps me exca-
vate a subterranean part of myself and my family. It helps me recover something lost in the transformations of 20th-century life, allows me to trace the
journey *tsvishn dortn un do*, between there and here, and to measure the
distances traveled.

As befits my left-wing secular Jewish upbringing, I reject any suggestion that this might be a mystical longing based on any racial or archetypal
urge. No. I am tapping into a genuine linguistic residue within myself. It's
there, in rhythms and inflections of speech, in attitudes and values that color
my perceptions and my most instinctive reactions. It's there in the songs
whose words are etched into my memory. And it's there in remembered
snatches of *heymish* conversation that somehow conveyed to a child the faint
essence of a whole world.

Acknowledgment. A *hartskin dank* to Paula Teitelbaum for help with
Yiddish transliteration and for her warm encouragement.

References

Forman, F., Raicus, E., Swartz, S. S., Wolfe, M. (Eds.). (1994). *Found treasures: Stories
by Yiddish women writers*. Toronto: Second Story Press.
Howe, I. (1976). *World of our fathers: The journey of the East European Jews to America
and the life they made and found*. New York: Harcourt Brace Jovanovich.
Schaechter-Gottesman, B. (1990). *Zumerteg (Summer days): Twenty Yiddish songs*.
New York: Congress for Jewish Culture and The League for Yiddish.

12

Language Is More than Words

SUSAN DRISCOLL

My acquisition of the Korean language has changed in meaning, purpose, and necessity throughout my life. For me, Korean represents far more than a second or foreign language. The process of my learning to speak Korean developed parallel to my quest for an identity. Learning Korean has been both a positive challenge and a personal struggle in my life.

In the 1960's my father was one of the first volunteers in South Korea in the Peace Corps. He worked there as an English teacher. My father fell in love with Korea, its culture and people, so he made the effort to learn everything that he possibly could about it, its history, customs, and language. By no coincidence, my mother became one of his students and they too fell in love. After my parents married in Pusan, the second-largest major city, they settled in the suburbs of New York where they raised their three daughters, me being the eldest.

Our town was small and somewhat closed off from the outside world. The people didn't venture much farther than Myrtle Beach, South Carolina for vacations and couldn't differentiate between Korea, China, and Japan. There was one supermarket with five aisles, one dentist, one doctor, one lawyer, two churches, one swimming pool, and one baseball field. My father chose this town because he felt it would be a comforting environment for my mother to make her transition into the American culture. The town was surrounded by high mountains, the way it was in her homeland.

There weren't any other Korean families in our small town. My parents had a few Korean friends and relatives living in the United States who would visit us from far away or vice versa. I wasn't exposed to the Korean language on a regular basis. The only spoken Korean I knew was some commonly used words, phrases, and songs that my mother had taught me.

I didn't know why we used these different-sounding words and songs in our house. To me, they were very strange and set our family apart from the "normal" American family. I often complained to my mother that she didn't do things the "right" way. As a child, I argued with her about eating smelly Korean foods when my friends came over to the house. Once I even asked my father why he couldn't find us a mommy with blonde hair and blue eyes.

When I was 11 years old the American economy was going into a slump and my father was laid off from his job. My parents had always wanted my sisters and I to learn about my mother's Korean culture and language while we were still young and developing our identities. At the time, we really had no idea what to expect from this move. We never thought that we would be going to this country called "Korea" that we had heard so much about. It was always a place only seen in pictures and talked about when other Koreans visited the house.

As soon as we arrived in Korea I learned that there was a place in the world where most of the people were speaking the same language as my mother and, interestingly enough, they were all like her in many ways! They laughed at the same jokes, they enjoyed eating the same types of food, and they talked about their children constantly in the same manner she did. The people in this country looked similar to my mother with their black hair and golden complexions. Also, the women's behavior was similar to my mother's, such as chuckling when they were nervous and giving the agreeing response "*nae*," which means "yes" or "I understand." I always thought that my mother was from some other planet where they ate foods that no one in New York ever heard of and sang strange songs that no one but my parents knew.

Our family lived in Korea for about two years. I enrolled in a Korean public school, where I made Korean friends and participated in daily school activities. In the beginning this was a very foreign experience to me. Not only was everything and everyone around me different from the United States, but I also knew that there was something that alienated me from everyone around me.

People were surprised to see how quickly I learned to speak Korean. My grandparents, aunts, and uncles were delighted to see their little American relative sounding more like them. I made very good friends at school and in our neighborhood whom I played with every day. I had no choice but to learn how to communicate as quickly as I could in order to live comfortably and feel somewhat like a normal kid.

After about two months of living in Korea, I began showing quick progress in speaking and listening. My mother taught my sisters and me how to read and write. We had Korean reading and writing lessons with her every day after school. After a lot of long hours and frustration, I learned to read and write fluently, although I could not follow all of the subjects in school like the other students. Music, art, and physical education were easier, but the other, more language-dependent subjects were challenging. I had private tutors at home to keep me consistent with all of my studies so as to not fall behind my grade level in the United States.

Within my first year in Korea, I spoke fluently and understood most of what was spoken around me. While my friends still treated me differently, I felt like I was one of them in many respects. We could communicate freely together in Korean. From time to time, they would ask me to translate something into English. I was very popular at school because I was "American." Everyone wanted to be my friend. Children I didn't even know would call my name or say hello to me in the schoolyard or on the street. The teachers asked me to lead their English lessons, which gave me my first interest in teaching English as a Second Language.

My sisters and I were essentially Korean in our actions and speech. However, the Koreans didn't always treat us as their equals. Korea is a very homogenous country, and any foreigner is easily noticeable to everyone. With our roundish eyes, pale complexions, and auburn hair, we soon became accustomed to receiving special attention from our teachers, friends, relatives, neighbors, and even strangers. We were often the center of attention both in and out of school. I was asked to give a short English lesson each morning to the entire school over the intercom and later wound up being interviewed on television about the differences between American and Korean school life. This certainly made our lives more exciting than ever before.

Learning Korean was natural for me at that time. I was growing up in Korea and I needed to speak the language in order to survive in school and society. It did not take long for me to acquire Korean because I heard and spoke it every day. It was like being a newborn child and having to acquire the language of the unfamiliar world around me. Not only did I learn to speak Korean, I also learned to *be* Korean. The Korean language is very complicated because in order to speak it correctly one must also know the social rules of the culture. For example, I always had to speak to my grandparents in the polite form in which every other question ended with "yo" (i.e., "*Mool mashilaeyo?*" means "Would you like a drink of water?") and statements ended with "da" (i.e., "*Illjik eelunasubnida*" means "I woke up early"). If I didn't follow the rules of the language, I would immediately feel the disapproval of the elders with whom I was speaking. I often made mistakes by not using the polite form with teachers and parents of friends. I learned through many embarrassing moments how and when to use the correct forms of the language.

Eventually, I became adjusted and led a typical Korean child's way of life. I played kickball, did my homework, walked to and from school, wore a gym uniform, ate a *"doshilak"* (Korean box lunch) at school, had my friends over to the house as well as played at their houses, wore my hair in pretty hair ties and clips, read comic books, received extra tutoring after school, watched Korean cartoons, rode the public buses to go to nearby places, and climbed a mountain with my parents on the weekends.

When my parents told my sisters and I that we were returning to the States we were ecstatic and saddened at the same time! At first, all I could think about was seeing my friends again, whom I had been writing to devotedly for nearly two years. When it came to the week of our departure I realized that my Korean friends and relatives were just as important to me as my American ones.

My identity crisis and temporary loss of a language came when our family returned to the United States at the beginning of my adolescence. I was reunited with my American friends and reentered our local Catholic school in the seventh grade. In the beginning, I experienced pretty bad culture shock. My American friends seemed more mature, independent, and self-conscious than I or my Korean friends were. I could also see that they were critical of me and my being different from them even more so than before I moved to Korea. They suggested that I not wear my hair in pigtails anymore and put on some makeup. In order to be accepted, I had to transform myself quickly from a Korean kid into an American teenager. That meant forcing myself to forget about my Korean identity as well as the language. It wasn't "cool" for me to be Korean. At that age, it was most important for me to fit in and conform to what all of the other kids were doing. I rarely spoke Korean, and when I did, I would only do so around my family and Korean relatives in private. I was embarrassed and ashamed of being Korean around my friends. Little by little, my use of Korean ceased almost completely. I only spoke it when it was absolutely necessary, such as when my grandmother asked me questions at home. Even then it was painful for me because of my stubborn American teenage ego. To me, the Korean language had become some kind of disease that I thought would make me sick.

I was often scolded for being a disrespectful Korean granddaughter. I only wanted to be "normal" and well-liked, as most teenagers do. However, the scolding became an everyday routine when I didn't acknowledge my grandmother's presence around the house or show her the respect that she naturally expected from all of her children and grandchildren. I was breaking the most important Korean customs, not to mention my grandmother's heart. This went on all through college, where I experienced the all-too-well-known scenes of sorority and fraternity social gatherings. I continued to be the typical all-American college woman away from home, starting her own life of independence.

Two weeks after my graduation party, with a bachelor's degree in English literature, I returned to Korea on my own. My sister had been back several times during summer vacations, but I was always making excuses that I was too busy with friends or college summer sessions. I went there with no expectations or agenda other than living with a wealthy family while teaching English to their only son and visiting relatives. I thought this would be the time for me to earn money and get some good life experiences. It had been 10 years since I lived there as a girl, so I didn't quite know what to expect. I was a little anxious because I hadn't spoken Korean regularly for all of those years living in the United States.

The moment I arrived at Korea's Kimpo International Airport in Seoul, to my own surprise, I began conversing with a man at the baggage counter in Korean. I caught myself off guard when the words began to naturally pour out from my mouth, Korean accent and all! It was as if I had instantly become Korean again! Oddly, I felt very comfortable in my new surroundings, as if I were arriving home.

For the first three months, I lived with a wealthy Korean family with whom I conversed in English in exchange for room, board, and a generous monthly allowance. I found living with them somewhat formal and uncomfortable. It seemed that I was there because they could afford to have me and that I was another household employee like their maid or chauffeur. I didn't have much opportunity to practice speaking Korean in their house because I was often left alone. In addition, I felt awkward speaking to them in English when they didn't know what I was saying most of the time. After the live-in private tutoring experience, I decided to teach English as a foreign language at a cram school for one year.

I moved into an apartment with three Korean girls who were my age. We immediately became friends and spent hours talking to each other about the differences between American and Korean cultures, values, and social behaviors. From our conversations, I gained many new perspectives on the ways of Korean people as well as a natural tongue and ear for the language. I was amazed at how quickly and accurately I relearned the Korean language. At times, I actually felt more Korean than American. I picked up a lot of slang and speech habits from the girls as we spent late hours together exchanging bits of cultural insight and interesting stories.

It came to be that the only time I spoke in English was with my students in my English classes and occasionally when I got together with other American teachers. Strangely enough, I felt more comfortable talking and doing things with my Korean friends than with the other Americans. I often stumbled over my words in English during conversations with

Americans because I was so used to speaking in Korean most of the time. I found that I was very different from the Americans I met in Korea. In our conversations, I didn't feel the same way about Korea as they seemed to. I often met Americans who spoke negatively about their Korean students or emphasized the fact that they were only going to stay in Korea until they made enough money to pay back their loans back home. I always felt a huge gap between myself and them. However, I was fortunate to meet a handful of American friends who were genuinely interested in being in Korea because they wanted to know the culture and language.

After about six months of sharing a home with the Korean girls, not only did my Korean speech become much more authentic, I also felt peaceful with my Korean identity for the first time.

Once when my mother called from the United States to speak to me, she mistook me for one of my Korean roommates. We often spoke to each other in Korean for lengths of time. This was unusual for us because we had been used to an English-speaking relationship. It felt like we were two different people when we spoke in Korean together. It must have been a joy for my Korean mother to speak to her American daughter in her mother tongue. By communicating in Korean, we connected in a way that had never been known to us, yet neither of us could or felt we had to explain it. For me, it was like discovering a whole new side of myself, or perhaps rediscovering what I had been so out of touch with for years, since I was a girl.

When I returned to the States after my year of teaching, my mother's Korean family and friends could hardly believe their ears and eyes when I spoke to them in Korean. I was no longer confused about what it meant for me to be Korean, nor was I ashamed of saying that I was Korean American. I finally felt good about my bicultural background, whereas in the past it was some kind of curse. Before, being Korean and American made my life painful and confusing. Now it made my life so much more exciting, fun, and full of many good surprises. I became aware of all of the advantages that I had. I realized that I had more opportunities than people who spoke only one language and knew of only one culture.

I continue to practice speaking Korean as often as I can with my mother, Korean relatives, grocers, tourists, friends, whenever the opportunity arises. I don't want to lose my Korean-speaking ability again. It is not a foreign language to me any longer. It is a very meaningful language that I associate with who I am and where I come from.

13

Learning My Native Language

SUSAN STOCKER

I vividly recall getting into a verbal tussle with my father when I was three or four years old. He thought he was distinctly saying the word "legs," but I kept hearing the word "eggs." He said, "legs." "Eggs," I thought I was repeating. "Legs," he said louder. "Eggs!" I responded. "Legs!!" Although I recognized his ominous tone, I was utterly clueless of what I might be doing wrong. My mother finally broke in with, "She can't hear you, Jack." Then he relented. Then he understood. And so did I. There was *something* I was missing.

I have been partly deaf since birth or early infancy. When I was four years old, doctors determined the precise level of my hearing impairment. My sensorineural loss is profound in the mid- to high-frequency range, which includes, in addition to crickets and most birdcalls, approximately half of the sounds that make speech meaningful. This is evident from my hearing chart, which shows a precipitous drop about halfway through the so-called "speech banana," the fat elongated upward-curving shape that depicts the range of human speech sounds. I can hear most vowels because they are low-frequency sounds, but there are some vowels and many consonants that I cannot hear because they are high-frequency sounds. To understand speech well, one must also discern these sounds because they contribute the acoustical nuances necessary to discriminate words and therefore meaning.

A person usually learns how to talk by imitating the speech patterns of those around her. This works well as long as one can take in the full contours of what those patterns are. When I first learned to speak, I simply did not reproduce the sounds I could not hear. How could I? I was palpably aware, of course, that my speech didn't sound right. Other children would make fun of the way I spoke. Or they would turn to their parents in my presence and ask what was wrong: "Why does she talk so funny?" I came to expect a certain level of pained embarrassment in the presence of other children, at least those whom I didn't know, but I was stunned when an adult once publicly called attention to my speech deficiency. I was about age 11 when I tried out for a theater production whose cast was to be comprised entirely of children. The adult director described to us the various characters in the play, which besides the typical male and female leads also had three spinners who spun wool. We fell into discussing the various parts for which we might try out. At this point, the director pointed to me and said that I could *only* try out for the spinner who had a harelip.

Linguistic competence is both an important condition for and marker of cultural belonging. What happens when the very medium of one's participation in her culture is fraught with uncertainty, guesswork, even shame? This was my experience of learning English, my native language.

Anticipating the Mainstream

My mother never let on that I couldn't do anything, or that things might be extra hard for me. Her belief in my abilities was, for such a long time, a prosthesis that I had to grow into on my own terms. Her constant refrain was "You can do it!" and again and again it filled me with renewed confidence; I believed it completely. Or so I thought. Only in hindsight do I realize how and why I so desperately welcomed this reassurance, because it spoke directly to my fear that I couldn't, in fact, "do it." I developed a wariness of activities that required verbal participation. After all, I knew that things were difficult, that I was missing lots of what transpired in the classroom and on the playground, and that because I almost never understood the words to songs, I was at a social disadvantage whenever references were made to the lyrics. All this put a real crimp in my otherwise abundant spontaneity and gregariousness. As a girl, I was paralyzed by embarrassment whenever I lost the crux of what was said.

My mother devoted a lot of time and energy to making sure that I had every opportunity to overcome my hearing deficiency. Long before I was old enough to pursue speech therapy, she taught me to lip-read by creating a game in which I was to get out of the bathtub by the time she counted to 10. Using only her lips, she counted along so that I would learn to gather visual cues. Over the years of my childhood, she also sought out a variety of different speech therapists whose approaches varied from having me practice sounds beyond my hearing range, difficult to reproduce without very specific coaching, to reciting memorized monologues with exaggerated enunciation. One of these recitations involved the phrase, "Loook aat thaaat flyyy oon thaaat baaaald-heeaadded maan's heeead." The idea was that overenunciation would likely settle into near-normal articulation.

But I spent most of those many years in speech therapy learning to reproduce sounds that were and remained mysterious to me. I had to be taught how to form my mouth and lips to sound the letters "r," "s," "sh," and "ch," all sounds I cannot hear. I remember one therapist who stuck a sharpened pencil in the small gap formed when the two front sets of incisors come together to form the letter "s." She would sit there with her pencil point inserted in that gap as I labored to recite a list of "s" words: *sly, soup, sale, simple, silly*. I went home from each session with lists of hard words to practice. I had to say them in front of a mirror to make sure my lips and tongue were positioned correctly.

The "ch" sound was next in difficulty. Here's the mechanical explanation: begin with the teeth together, the lips formed as though an "s" were coming, but after the "s" is started, finish up the sound with an explosive force of air behind the teeth as they then open and the tongue comes down from the roof of the mouth. As if doing all of that were not enough, I still had to say the rest of the word! Then, having taught me to form these sounds, various speech therapists still had to stress how important they were to use. Despite all this training, I am told that my speech retains a slight flatness that endures beneath the inflections.

Nearly Drowning in the Mainstream

I remember being humiliated in the first grade on a multiple-choice test. Question: what sound does a fire make? The choices: a) hiss, b) pop, and something unmemorable like c) whine. Based on my own experience, I chose "pop." I had heard a fire do that. But the teacher said that the correct answer was "hiss," singling me out and chastising me in front of the class for choosing an incorrect answer. I felt both shamed and unjustly accused—with a child's fine sense of injustice. So, in an attempt at retributive justice, I later hid the classroom pencil sharpener container.

In the sixth grade, however, I actually experienced an advantage from my deafness. My teacher's name was Miss Cleare. Unlike my fifth grade teacher, whose confidence and ready humor had won our affection, this teacher inspired aversion. But I never meant to ridicule her when I mistakenly called her "Miss Queer." That's how I heard her name. My classmates, of course, were giddy with the thought that I was being sassy. For the first time in my life, I was suddenly popular with the whole class! Although I always had close friends, I had never felt comfortable in large groups. There were just too many important verbal clues I knew I could be missing. By the time I caught on that "Miss Queer" was not really her name, my elevated social status was secured.

As I got older, in junior high school, I geared myself up for the emotional challenges of deafness. I set out to assuage my own terror of being inadequate by compensating with unrealistically high standards for myself. Good enough just wasn't good enough. I found I could do everything well in the domain of physical activities. I practiced my basketball shots, spending hours on the court by myself with an obsessive draconian system—a sports superego. I had to make 10 shots in a row from each one of a dozen designated stations on the court before I could move on. Between missed shots, I would chastise myself and vow to do better.

So for many years my achievements were athletic; I brought a laser intensity to learning these skills. But in classes, even participation remained very difficult. I could only hear about three-quarters of what was said. Being too ashamed to interrupt the class to ask for repetition, I would grow frustrated and feel isolated. Then I would space out, and top it all off by feeling guilty for spacing out. Even though Mother told me to sit up front and raise my hand whenever I missed something, the prospect of revealing my disability was too searing even to consider.

I really didn't know how to acknowledge or cope with my secret feelings of frustration, isolation, inadequacy, and terror. I kept these secrets from my mother as much as I could. Ironically, my mother's dedication to do everything she could gave me—I suspect—the sense that underneath her encouragement, she might be as concerned as I about just how it would go. So I felt it incumbent upon me to achieve at a high level, not only to convince myself, but to justify her confidence.

By the time I graduated from college I had developed a style of working on academic matters that reflected my drivenness on the basketball court. I merely extended my modus operandi. Superficially, this driven style of working proved to be very successful. It enabled me not only to finish college, but to go on to earn three graduate degrees. I grew to love those periods of intense focus when my mind flooded with questions, ideas, connections, prospects. At the same time, however, the determined nature of my work impeded my development of a repertoire of sustainable, flexible working styles that would support a more humane life. I was always at full-court press, lacking a rhythm or joy in drawing from other parts of my soul.

In my late 20s, I took a sign language course at Gallaudet University for the Deaf, an environment that favors the profoundly deaf. The congenitally deaf teacher would pronounce the words as she signed them. Not only was her tone very flat, she underpronounced the words. Between not being able to make out her speech and still struggling to recognize the signs, I had trouble making sense of the information conveyed in the classroom, which struck me as ironic in this very pro-Deaf environment. Despite this, and more important than the sign language I did manage to pick up, I learned something valuable. The teacher displayed a shining sense of entitlement. She was unapologetically Deaf-identified. She even had something of a chauvinistic attitude toward the hearing, which for the first time included me. I was at once stung by it and yet arrested by her confidence.

In seeking out this environment, I suppose I was looking for some indigenous setting, a lost home, the way an adopted friend sought out his biological parents once he finished college. Like him, I discovered that as difficult as it was, I was grateful for the way things turned out for me. Having revisited the choices my parents had made on my behalf, I was glad to have been mainstreamed to participate in the wide world. But I was struck by the in-between character of being hard of hearing: we're not hearing and we're not Deaf. Having learned that I didn't really belong in the deaf community, I was still negotiating that wider world.

In addition to shaping my work habits, the accumulated experience of my deafness was such a "hot stove" emotionally that even into my 30s, anytime I got near it I felt burned. I was often exasperated and exhausted, wanting so much to be able to hear what was going on. Increasingly, I had bouts of helplessness and hopelessness, usually after some social event in which I desperately wanted to participate, and strained to hear, but simply lost some crucial clues. Or at least, I feared that what I had lost was the crucial part. And sometimes it clearly was. That's just it, you never know for sure.

The most wrenching incident took place during one summer during graduate school at St. John's College. I had been invited to the home of some fellow students, together with a beloved faculty member. We were sitting outside in a courtyard underneath the immense New Mexico sky. It was one of those thrilling conversations that I live for. I was a relative newcomer to philosophy and the conversation turned to the topic I most wanted to discuss and hear about—the comparison between Plato and Aristotle. Unfortunately, just at this point, the sun began to set. As it grew too dark for me to read lips, I was filled with mute anguish. More than anything I wanted to be in on that conversation. After returning to campus, I paced around mourning my loss and crying out of sheer frustration.

Each such incident tapped into this growing reservoir of pain and isolation. I sank down into a deeper and deeper well that reverberated with anger, frustration, guilt, and shame. Why shame? Perhaps because we're most ashamed of what we can't help.

During graduate school, I began psychotherapy, where I relived many similarly painful episodes. From experiencing my therapist's empathy for my struggle, I began to learn self-empathy. Slowly, this enabled me to reframe my situation, to modify what I could and to accept the things I couldn't. Once I became more comfortable with my own limits, the heat of that hot stove began to dissipate. To those closest to me, I began to explain my angst over not being able to hear well enough to participate in certain settings. I discovered that the people who care for me not only accept my conditions for participation, but even help to secure them, for instance, by turning down the background music when I arrive. I grew easier with the fact that I have certain nonnegotiable conditions for being able to participate in conversation. The restaurant has to be quiet and well lighted; I have to be able to see the lips of the person speaking, no screening hand gestures. Given this ease within my intimate circle, I was able to negotiate other arenas more easily.

As a college professor, I always mention my impairment on the first day of class, so the students will understand if I should ask them to repeat things. As a result, the disabled students come up to me after class and inform me of their respective challenges. Because it fosters an ease in them, this explicit embrace of my own limits is an asset. In short, I can now generally respond to most situations without tapping into the whole legacy of my past pain. I still miss hearing things, of course, and struggle with it. But the backlog of pain has dissolved and the pangs I feel are mostly attributable to the incident at hand.

Mainly Streaming

Now that I have accommodated myself emotionally to my hearing deficiency, I often laugh at my zany interpolations and invite my friends to share my amusement. This usually happens because of the way I mentally run through acoustical possibilities whenever I hear something I can't quite decipher. Not infrequently I find myself in the presence of a meaning that, albeit acoustically close, is quite different from what the speaker meant. Last year I introduced someone to a colleague who subsequently commented that this ruddy-looking individual was "a tanning bed person." Based on what I "heard," I asked how she knew that that person was "a ten in bed." She laughed, "Yep, I can just look at someone and tell." Then she wryly added, "and it saves me a lot of time!"

Even with this newfound playfulness, my punishing work style has continued. In fact, only in the past two years—I'm now 46—have I gained any critical insight about the ways my strategies for hearing were translated into strategies for living. As a child, I felt personally responsible for facing my hearing challenges, because, after all, there was nothing I couldn't do "if I really put my mind to it." But the modality I developed is over-determined: Put a challenge in front of me and I'll try to overcome it. Struggle became so familiar and comfortable a mode that unless engaged in an ordeal, I mistrusted myself. I feared I wasn't doing my best work. An academic career nourished this crazed drivenness. Although I genuinely love philosophy, academic work also held out for me the prospect of finally attaining in the domain of the written word the exhaustiveness that so eluded me in spoken speech.

But this drivenness trapped me. In a variety of ways, my body and psyche began to rebel against this regime. Moreover, I became concerned about what my lifestyle was modeling for my students. Is this—and nothing less—required to have a career or to be a philosopher? A colleague sent me a quote by Alfred Mercier: "What we learn with pleasure, we never forget." I taped it above my computer screen. While I am still unlearning the determined drivenness I used to rely on to meet the challenges of being mainstreamed in the hearing world, I can look up and breathe. I am also learning to cultivate a certain receptivity in my work, a shift that enriches it beyond what a full-tilt effort produces.

Because learning my native language has been so arduous, it has shaped my identity in complex ways, both redemptive and constraining. What I've learned from reading accounts of midlife course corrections, however, is how common it is for middle-aged people to rethink the strategies that got them through their childhood and early adulthood. While granting us a form of knowledge, our professional training can too often close us to the moves we actually need to use to live vital adult lives. Those abilities from which we derive professional recognition can become so sharpened as to suppress other indispensable parts of our souls.

Perhaps my story is a variation on a theme that I am just beginning "to hear." When what helped me had helped me enough, its efficacy began to shrink and then to spoil. Now that I can sometimes see challenges as foolish and refuse some of them, I have choices about how to direct my skill and energy. I can have more joy in a myriad of things that don't speak as evidence of my value but give me a richer intellectual, aesthetic, and relational world. I can play without a scorecard, as it were. I also recognize that certain settings trigger my tendency to fall back on obsessive "proving myself" behaviors. And I can name this and set these tasks aside. Acquiring this liberty is one of the joys of language.

Acknowledgments. I want to express my heartfelt thanks to those who reviewed earlier versions of this chapter and made useful suggestions: Betty Smith Franklin, Ashby Sharp, Dan Davis, Barbara Roswell, and Kathy Wood. My thanks also go to Rick Pringle, who invited me to present a version of this piece in his class on Perception.

14

Recollections

MARGIE ENGLISH

It was a thrilling day for my parents when they found out they had a Deaf daughter; they never pictured themselves having an extended Deaf family. My parents felt so much joy in their good fortune that they felt uncomfortable about sending me to a far-off school. My parents went to the North Carolina School for the Deaf in Morganton, N.C. They grew up distanced from their own families, and they did not want the same fate for their Deaf children. My parents held good jobs and lived in the Washington area, which is several hundred miles away from the Virginia School for the Deaf and Blind. They decided to send me to a nearby oral school named Camelot. By that time, my brother, also Deaf, had been born.

I spent my prekindergarten years receiving speech lessons and running around. Apparently I did not understand the purpose of school, other than playing. Mom noticed that I arrived home every afternoon looking depressed. At home, I could talk all I wanted in American Sign Language, but at school, I was punished for signing. After school, I would not talk about what happened that day, but instead, I would run to my room and play with Barbies.

My parents realized their mistake in sending me to Camelot. They moved heaven and hell to enroll my brother and me in Kendall School, a school for the Deaf located on the same campus as Gallaudet University. By autumn 1980, at age four, I walked into Kendall on the first day of school and was overwhelmed. The school was beautiful! The halls were colorful, and all the kids signed! I loved my class, full of kids with flying hands! I had fun meeting new friends and writing down their names so I could remember them. As soon as I settled in, I continued to divert my attention to play. Perhaps I was basking in the newfound delight of being able to use my hands without any restrictions. The teacher of that young class noticed that I was not making any progress. She determined that I was slow and needed special attention in the classroom.

My parents were upset at my transfer to a special class, for they knew I had good vocabulary. As Deaf parents, Mom and Dad took advantage to teach us new words through ASL. Mom signed out biblical stories and other stories from books, while Dad held somber conversations with us. My brother and I, and later my little sister, also Deaf, sat next to Mom while she recreated the stories through her hands into a three-dimensional world playing around us. We peeked into the books whenever we wanted to see a face of a character or a clearer image of the setting, while Mom kept on signing. Sometimes we jumped in with questions or comments, which Mom fielded or referred to Dad for better answers. Mom later said she always enjoyed seeing how small and cute her children's hands were when we first started signing.

Immediately after arriving home from the meeting that determined my transfer to another class, Mom made me spell out things she pointed at. I answered all of them correctly, yet I did not touch my list of new words on the blackboard at school. Mom then stuck masking tape on various items around the house and wrote their names on it. Among the words I remember are "window" on the glass panes of a window, and "fish" on the fish tank holding five goldfishes. Mom drilled into me the importance of telling the teacher what I'd learned. After several weeks and multiple temper tantrums, I returned to my original class.

Next came my teacher in second grade, Jean Slobodzian, who encouraged our class to investigate new areas of knowledge. She set aside 30 minutes daily for us to write, and she told us to "write anything you want. Be creative!" The pages we wrote on were divided into halves; the top half was left blank for drawings and the bottom half had lines to guide our letter placement. We also scribbled our thoughts and feelings about the class into our dialogue journals every morning. Not only did Jean make us write, but she also encouraged us to read. She sat the class in a semicircle and read to us the Paddington Bear series. After a while, I began to look forward to the times when I would be able to either create or listen to a story.

Even if I adored stories, reading them terrified me. I preferred having adults retell stories to me. I guess the size of the book and the number of words scared me. This fear continued until I, at age eight, slept over at a Deaf friend's place. I was playing downstairs when I noticed my friend was missing. I looked for her until I found her holed up on a sofa with a gigantic book. The book looked as if it had more than a thousand pages! I stared at her with awe and asked, "Can you really read that?" My friend got perturbed, and she told me that I could do the same. Not really believing her,

I tried a book without pictures for the first time, and I realized I understood words in it! I felt like I had accomplished something great.

By the time I was nine, I was a confirmed bookworm. Books were a source of fascinating information and ideas, and I gobbled them up. I felt a secret pleasure every time a person learned something from me that I had recently read about. Vocabulary became a major part of my life. I did not want to limit myself to the same words every time I wrote, so I fed myself with new words and learned how to use them. As I was doing that, I learned how to check through my drafts for structural and grammatical errors. At approximately the same time, I got my first diary. I became a loyal entry writer, because I loved the idea of having my own children read my words when I become ancient. Being a novice writer, I attempted my first story. It was about a girl who was murdered and became a ghost who haunted the site of her own murder. I worked diligently on this story until I became bored with it, and started another story; thus, I became a writer with loads of ideas but without commitment.

Throughout elementary school, I always took speech lessons. My classmates nudged each other about the possibility of speech teachers nodding and saying "good!" even when we couldn't accurately form words with our tongues. My speech teacher always praised me each time I finished a lesson, and I didn't believe her. One afternoon, I asked her if she was being truthful in her praises, and she told me that I formed words with my mouth well, but I would need to practice making sounds with my nose and I forget what other places, too. I knew I had a Deaf voice, flat and without tone. I was so proud of being Deaf that I told my parents in my wonderful visual language that I didn't want to continue my speech lessons in eighth grade. I preferred to look goofy trying to gesture an idea to a non-Deaf person rather than sound goofy trying to speak it; that way, I could deal with the picture I created, because that was something I understood, as compared to the sounds I could not hear myself create. My parents didn't mind one way or another, so they arranged for me not to have to take those lessons. When I returned to finish the last year of elementary school, my speech teacher confronted me. She asked me point-blank: "Why are you not taking speech lessons this year?" I answered, "Because I don't want to." She gave me a disgusted look, and I walked away.

High school brightly opened a new world for me. I began to critically analyze literary writings, absorbing ideas like a sponge. I could not wait to try out new techniques in my writing that I learned from reading literature in class. Our class discussed various topics through ASL, which allowed us to retrieve visual ideas stored in our brains and spin them out through our fingers. The class discussions always helped with students' understanding of the subject at hand. The teachers were able to provide constructive feedback and ideas for discussion; they were capable of presenting complicated ideas through our native language and displaying intensive knowledge of the subject. Every now and then, we had a novice signer as a teacher or a teacher-substitute, and those teaching staff either learned to sign our language better, or moved into another field. To excel, we required the best teachers available who could communicate fluently in ASL, and we knew that not many schools for Deaf students were able to provide this privilege.

Model Secondary School for the Deaf (MSSD) encouraged free writing, which promoted improvements in our usage of English through feedback during peer review. To meet MSSD's free writing requirement, I joined a public electronic bulletin board on Prodigy named the Guenther's Academy. Friends who frequented this board were encouraged to post their written work. They were also expected to offer constructive feedback on various pieces of work each individual posted. These friends helped me develop stories and poetry that got published in the MSSD literary magazine, *Aerie*. Later, fellow writers and I created fantasies together. We took turns writing the thoughts and feelings of our characters, allowing these to guide the story. It was a good experience working with other writers, and I felt as if I could write about anything I wanted.

A scholar from Chicago, Paul, who also frequented Guenther's Academy, learned that I was Deaf and for his New Year's resolution, he wanted to learn how to sign. Paul came to D.C. for a weeklong visit, and we struggled through the basics of ASL. He had practiced at home, but when we met face-to-face, all signs he had learned flew out of his memory. Paul spent more time that week learning about how I saw things as a Deaf person than learning ASL. At one point, he asked me if I would marry a hearing man if I loved one. I didn't need to think about it; I wanted to marry a Deaf guy who I could talk with about anything, and not worry about being misunderstood because of a sloppily signed word. Paul accused me of discrimination, and this issue later broke our friendship. I worried if my position on this issue was wrong until I realized that I only needed to feel comfortable communicating with the man I loved. If that's discrimination, then so be it. One can be discriminating when it comes to choosing life mates. Life goes on.

During my senior year, I took courses in modern novels and classical literature at Gonzaga, a private Catholic all-boys preparatory school. The idea of being one of two girls in an entirely male classroom daunted me. Babar, also my roommate at MSSD, and I spent a nervous week getting used to Ms. Free, the teacher all the boys ogled. She expected a response paper to each novel we completed. Babar and I weren't sure how to write a brief essay. We were used to lengthy research papers full of run-on sentences, but Ms. Free only asked for one to two pages of essay. "You don't know how to write a five-paragraph essay?" Ms. Free exclaimed when we asked how she wanted the essay to look like. We felt stupid while she jotted down the general outline, including specific requirements for the intro- duction. Babar and I gave each other pep talks while we wrote our first essays for Ms. Free. We hoped our English skills would not fail us, espe- cially with a new audience who ate, slept, and thought in native English. I learned how to develop comprehensive answers and essays. By the end of the year, I felt more comfortable with expressing my thoughts on paper.

Throughout the year at Gonzaga, we had uncertified interpreters who tried to learn how to become professionals. Those amateurs were students who hoped to become certified translators for the Deaf community. Some wore distracting long nails with bizarre polishes, and others lost deco- rum whenever we looked down to write notes and/or read passages Ms. Free was reading aloud. My favorite "terp" was a man who kept on kick- ing either Babar's desk or mine when we persisted in keeping our heads down. It was because of him that we kept creating new ways to annoy him. Later, we reduced ourselves to giggling whenever we saw him sign a nonsensical word.

I wonder if Ms. Free realized that we did not understand her lectures at all, but that we made do with the literature we already had with us? Now, I would kick myself if I let an interpreter go on and on without any warn- ing that I did not understand what was being said. Sometimes, it still feels weird communicating through an interpreter. With my current work as an employment specialist, I interact with both Deaf and hearing people, in- cluding interpreters. I didn't realize how hard it is to become a certified interpreter, and how much courage it requires to foray into a new com- munity. Imagine yourself listening to continuous sentences in one language and translating them into continuous sentences in another language, think- ing simultaneously in two languages. At college, I experimented with inter- preting for the Deaf-Blind in classes, but I was merely offering my hands for language comprehension, and not actually translating one language to another. I thank interpreters for their continuous support of the Deaf com- munity, which requires a huge bilingual and bicultural role.

After I graduated from MSSD, I entered Gallaudet University. Whoa! That sure was a blast! During my elementary years, I had picked up an array of unnecessary Anglicized signs that just wouldn't go away until I came to Gallaudet. My classmates, thank goodness, had no reservations about pointing them out. I have since changed the way I sign *apple*, thank you, Bonnie. I majored in English, and wish I had also majored in ASL. (I made the mistake of waiting until I finished most of my credits to take courses related to ASL). Gallaudet offers the Deaf community a liberal arts education with all the fringe benefits, minus the barriers experienced with living in a mainstream community. Gallaudet has many courses available for students who are willing to challenge themselves by meeting new ideas. Many organizations complement Gallaudet's plentiful offerings: Student Body Government, Student Congress, Buff-N-Blue, Tower Clock, Drama, Gallaudet Dance Company, Black-Deaf Student Union, Asian-Pacific Association, Student Judicial Board, athletic sports, assorted fraternities and sororities, and many other clubs. Through the activities I participated in at Gallaudet, I realized that self-expression is a lifelong process in which each one of us will develop an individual style and ideas. I am always learning how to refine my ASL and am always finding better ways to improve my English.

Even today, with a bachelor's degree, I have to remind myself how to place words in a sentence. Actually, I don't think I'm different; my peers, Deaf or hearing, need to be careful about how they write words in English. My typical drafts have scribbles and crossed-out words on them. Often, when I try to organize a paragraph, I struggle with translating into English the ASL picture I have in my mind. Perhaps that's like how many hearing people sound out words while they write, the only difference being how our brains retrieve information, by sight or by sounds. It is easier for me to sign out my ideas than to write them down. Sometimes when I write, my words come out garbled, especially if I am in an ASL mindframe. If I sit down at a computer or a table in a quiet room, I can switch my mind to my "English" channel, and my sentences become easier to write. My crossouts become less obvious, but that doesn't stop me from making revisions when I type the next draft!

I have always perceived English as a challenge, for it is so auditory in nature, as compared to my native and picturesque American Sign Language. I enjoy dealing with the finer points of the complex languages I use on a daily basis. I shall forever be a student of both languages.

Part III

THE DIFFICULTIES OF LANGUAGE LEARNING

In this section, three native English-speaking Americans describe with great sensitivity how, while enjoying the sounds of other languages, they remain outside and unable to speak them. The pieces in this section reflect the irony of American privilege: While having access to an abundance of foreign culture, as a country, we remain one of the most linguistically deficient in the world.

Robert Roth traces much of his struggles to his father, a Hungarian Jewish immigrant who was never comfortable in English. Using a fragmented approach, Roth expresses his shifting locations inside, outside, and sometimes in between languages. He uses the form of his writing to convey how non-standard forms of language are not accepted for the positive and expressive qualities that they often have. He goes deep inside his own consciousness to explore both the positive and negative dimensions of his resistance to learning languages.

Sharon Shelton Colangelo largely attributes her inability to acquire Spanish, or any other foreign language, to the rote and physically constrictive method used to teach her in the public school she attended as a child in Texas. The sense of play and movement that she feels her foreign language education lacked speaks to the significance of the body in language learning, and the importance of maintaining this natural connection, even within the limited confines of a classroom.

Stephanie Hart relates her monolingualism to the harsh censorship of her father, a talented linguist who spoke many languages fluently. Her piece ends on a note of promise, however, as she reaches the epiphany that only after removing herself from the specter of her father's judgment, and allowing herself to be less than perfect, can she begin to open herself up to the world of language learning that has always held so much fascination for her.

15

Random Thoughts on My Inability to Learn Languages

ROBERT ROTH

1

I first saw Arnie, my oldest and dearest friend, at a Free Speech rally at Queens College in New York City during a student strike. I think it was in 1962. This beautiful and intense figure moved from person to person, group to group, listening, speaking, engaged in the event with a seriousness much different than anyone else seemed to have. It was as if a spotlight followed him everywhere he went. Wherever he stood, it seemed as if something historical was at stake.

The next time I saw Arnie was in Spanish class. He looked spaced out, dazed, lost in some deep internal chaos. The only person more spaced out than me. Each day we would go around the room and have to translate a sentence from English to Spanish. Arnie was always the ninth person called on. I was always the twelfth. Neither of us ever got the answer right. One day I saw that the translations were in the back of the book. So I started memorizing Answer 12. But Arnie never knew Answer 9. So it was really Answer 11 that I would have to give. Finally it dawned on me to memorize Answer 11. Of course, that was the one time Arnie got the answer right. To this day we have never figured out how he did it.

2

For nine years I went to Hebrew-speaking camp. Instead of learning Hebrew, I went off by myself shooting baskets. Even after 9 years, I could say maybe 25 words. I couldn't say something as simple as "Please pass the sugar." I could read Hebrew to a degree, though I didn't know what most of the words meant. This is true of many Jews who pray. They can say and chant the prayers but don't know the literal meaning of the words. For three years running I was given the same primer to study from in camp. The only thing different was the technique of the teachers. The warm, embracing, encouraging technique of one of the teachers, while no more successful in helping me learn a word, has, as I write this, left me with a fond memory. And possibly some regrets in the frustration I must have caused.

3

A friend from Japan entirely panicked at an anti-apartheid demonstration in Central Park. The sound system was awful. It was impossible to understand a word. She thought it was because her English was bad. Afterwards she just sat down in the street and started to cry. I've noticed that people when they're drunk or angry often speak a blue streak in a language that they otherwise might have difficulty with. I suspect that a person in a strange country during a moment of heightened sexual arousal might get various languages all jumbled together.

4

My father was a person not comfortable in any language. He came to the United States as a young boy from Hungary. He never really fully spoke Hungarian, though he was able to communicate okay in it. He never fully learned English, though he ran a business here. He was able to read newspapers and books in English. His problem was more in speaking and writing. He could read Hebrew, though for the most part he didn't understand the words. And he could speak a smidgen of Yiddish. I often wondered what language his thoughts were in.

My father had to rely on his smarts. If he didn't know mathematical formulas, he could add and subtract and multiply and divide very quickly in his head. For his purposes, this was good enough. There was a point, of course, where this wouldn't be sufficient. My cousin, a young and gifted mathematics professor, could not match my father in certain mathematical exercises. But by knowing the formulas, she could figure out certain problems that were way beyond the sheer force of my father's intelligence.

My mother was "better educated" than my father. She became an art historian. She writes English beautifully. And speaks fluently with a heavy Hungarian accent.

I think it is from my father, who by his wits could run circles around more "educated" people (I'm not talking about my mother here), that I developed some of my resistance to learning.

My resistance to language learning extends to computers, mathematics, physics, the social sciences, street slang, almost any and every language. Like my father, I can pick up things, just enough at times to get a sense of what is going on. But not enough to converse or move beyond the point where instinct and intuitive grasp can take me.

5

My problems with English, my native language, are pretty acute. Only every so often can I write anything that makes any sense. Usually it is incoherent fragments written in a totally illegible scrawl that even I can't read. The scrawl translates itself into incomprehensible combinations of letters if I'm attempting to write by typewriter rather than by hand. It is only very rarely that I am able to enter the space where I can communicate with written words. When I can, I can. It is almost as simple as that.

As I mentioned before, my father was never comfortable in any language. My friend Paula, on the other hand, seems more comfortable in Italian than in her native English. It is as if she had been born into the wrong language. I remember seeing her, actually spying on her from a distance, speaking Italian to a friend. Her hand gestures, her facial gestures, her body language seemed so much more at home in Italian than in English. I spoke to her about what I had observed. She said yes, it was true. It is amazing to see people and the changes they go through with the language that they're speaking, how their gestures, the timbre of their voice, the depth of their laughter, their body language are affected by the language they are speaking. Sometimes these changes occur from one moment to the next.

6

I was taught French in high school. I remember enjoying reciting a poem in class once.

Three years of Spanish in college. I visited Argentina a couple of years ago. Spanish made more sense there than in the classroom. In a limited way I was actually able to speak and understand it while I was there. I attend a poetry series in Brooklyn where a lot of the work is read in Spanish. While I don't understand much of what is read, I usually get real pleasure out of the event. This is also true of lectures and poetry readings in English, as well as various types of concerts. My mind rarely focuses in on what's in front of me. But often something important does enter my consciousness. This is why I'm never hurt if someone falls asleep at a reading I am giving.

I learned Hungarian from my cousin's mother as a child. My parents spoke English, not Hungarian, to each other at home. I think if I lived in Hungary for a year, Hungarian would be a language that I could learn to speak. I can understand it when my relatives speak it. I have a much harder time when strangers speak it.

Hebrew? I still can't speak it. My ability to read it has diminished. But when I go to the synagogue to mourn my dead father, the sounds of prayer connect me deeply to him.

As for speaking English, it astounds me when I hear myself on tape to think that anyone can understand a word I say. Mostly sounds, a few expletives, a few key words, a bunch of you-knows, and that's about it. People have to work hard. Maybe that's the key. Or you know maybe they just I don't know. Anyway.

16

The Promise of *Español*

SHARON SHELTON COLANGELO

It was just another day at school, one of those scorching late September days at the beginning of the semester when we squirmed in our chairs, uncomfortable in our new fall clothes and not yet used to sitting still after three months off. By third grade most of us had come to realize that this business of schooling involved little more than obeying; the magic of first grade—the paints, our Dick and Jane primers, the smells of our lunch boxes—had long since evaporated.

Ms. Greene was what we called a "pretty lady" and she had a nice smile, but already after two weeks of school we were hopelessly bored. It seemed like all we did was read out of our textbooks and start the process all over. We coped by writing notes, doodling on scraps of paper, and sometimes whispering when we thought she wasn't looking. I mostly daydreamed, mechanically carrying out whatever was wanted without even having to think much about it.

On this day, however, and just when I had a really good daydream going, one about being a little girl living in Montana, wearing all white, and riding a fast white horse, Ms. Greene surprised us by passing out little brown books entitled *Español, Español!* The word rolled off my tongue like a song. I learned that *Español* was what "people to our south" spoke, and we were going to learn to speak it, too! I was thrilled, and I noticed that even Jessie Robbins, the class clown who usually spent his time putting banana peels on his head and leaning on the hind legs of his chair, cocked his head forward with interest. We were going to learn *Español*, and the little brown books would help us.

I still remember the cream-colored pages of those books and the smell of their paper and ink. I learned how to say, "*¿Como esta usted?*" a question that had only one answer—"*Muy bien, gracias.*" Jessie and I took turns asking and answering that question over and over again.

"*¿Como esta usted?*"

"*Muy bien, gracias.*"

"*¿Como esta usted? . . .*"

This dialogue became a sort of ritualistic incantation where the sounds of the words meant as much or more than their meaning.

We had Spanish class only twice a week, but sometimes when we were working on multiplication or spelling, Jessie would suddenly lean my way with an impish look and whisper some of the wondrous words from our Spanish book: "*escuela,*" "*niños*" "*abuela,*" and, once, "*te amo.*" Sometimes I would make my own miniature book, sketching pictures of little cats and dogs, labeling them in Spanish, and shoving my handiwork across the desk for Jessie to inspect.

When we weren't studying Spanish, our textbooks lay neatly stacked on a shelf. I often gazed at them from my seat, longing to look at their brightly colored pictures. I loved the illustrations of little girls in long turquoise dresses and boys gallant in white pants under red-tiled roofs. One picture, Ms. Greene explained, showed a Mexican hat dance, and that very night I went home, turned on the radio, and demanded that my brothers and sister join me in repeatedly jumping over one of my father's old hats to the music. We were Mexican children, I decided, and we lived in a "*casa.*" We laughed and danced, and before going to sleep, I murmured to my sister, "*Buenos noches.*"

Today I can't recall much about Ms. Greene's methods of teaching Spanish, other than group recitations and probably lots of copying from our books. Yet I do remember how truly desperately I wanted to learn. Several times later, in 5th grade, in 10th and 11th grades, in college, and even once as an adult, I attempted to learn Spanish, but never with the same enthusiasm and absolute certainty that I could learn it, that I was learning it. Somehow over time, *Español,* too, had ceded its romance to the worksheets, and I began to look upon it like I did everything else in school.

As a teacher, I try to remind myself of the electric thrill that shot through my body so many years earlier at the prospect of speaking another language. I believe that most children have a natural curiosity and desire to communicate that is slowly suffocated by years of drill-and-skill training, aimed mostly at teaching obedience. As a child, I attempted on my own to communicate with my siblings and my peers through Spanish, that wondrous new language that I was encountering in school. Spontaneously, I tried to enter a culture other than my own through purposeful communication with my peers and through imaginative play, dance, and drama with my brothers and sister.

Instead of requiring students to copy out of books, complete work-sheets, and take tests, teachers need to devise more holistic and joyful activities that encourage learners to reconnect with their natural curiosity and to "try on" a culture and its language. We need to help students enter other worlds, try on new concepts and practices, and use their discoveries as the basis of which to grow, replacing lockstep drill with opportunities for active learning and critical reflection. I want my own students to dance, to draw, to daydream, to concoct narratives, to ponder, to play, to laugh, to experience pleasure as they learn—in just the same way that I did when I first encountered the promise of *Español*.

17

Why I Shouldn't Speak Only English

STEPHANIE HART

Grasping for Meanings

The landscape of a second language has always held a fascination for me. Each new terrain seems to echo with the spirit of the place and its people. On a recent trip to Europe, a friend and I traveled by bus up Spain's rocky northern coast. I watched giant pines climb beside us like conquistadors. In the distance a ruined castle leaned against the sky. The stark power of Castilian Spanish hovered on the wind, or so I imagined. I wanted to decipher those proud syllables, roll them off my tongue and explore their versatility. The spirit of Spain was very much alive on the bus. I heard it in the voices of families, elderly travelers, and most especially in the animated conversation of a young couple across from us. I remember the woman's long, inquisitive profile and the man's round bearded face that kept baring in a smile. Although I listened hungrily for fragments of meaning, I was unable to speak. Despite years of studying Spanish in both high school and college, my native language, English, was my only source of linguistic competence. Would I remain forever on the perimeter of other vistas?

I am the only member of my family who is monolingual. My father was a Russian immigrant who by the age of 20 had mastered not only English, but also German, Spanish, French, and Italian. As a student of philosophy and literature at Harvard, he studied the literature and syntax of all four languages. He took pride in his fluency, believing that his gift for nuance and idiom gave him access to other cultures and histories. Shortly before his death at 84, my father and stepmother traveled to Switzerland. I remember the gleam in his eyes as he told of his chameleon like adventures into Italian, French, and German. Passengers on buses and trolleys were convinced he was a native speaker of each language.

If You Can't Speak It Perfectly . . .

My father's love of languages permeated my early childhood. We lived in a house by the sea on the southern tip of New Jersey. At the age of six, I remember my father and I building sand castles on the beach. Dad would transport us to Spain and materialize as Don Quixote. He had taught me that Don Quixote was a chivalrous knight who battled both giants and pirates and could make absolutely anything happen just by thinking about it. In that spirit, Dad managed to metamorphose clouds into acrobats, and the sea into a magic carpet for us to fly on. He would swing me over his shoulders singing in a lilting, rhythmic Spanish, and I would laugh, offering my own rendition of the language. A cathedral of possibilities opened for me during these flights of fantasy, and they were inextricably linked with the Spanish language.

The tide of imagination extended to other languages during this period. My father was a devotee of the opera. He knew the scores of *Carmen*, *Madama Butterfly*, and *La Bohème* by heart. Dressed up in my mother's kimono, I would watch the sea through our picture window for Lieutenant Pinkerton's ship as the score to *Madama Butterfly* wafted through our living room. The music seemed to move through me and wrap itself around me. The grandeur and sadness of the Italian language gave me a passport to emotions I had never experienced.

Both my parents were fluent in Yiddish. I learned subliminally that this was a language I was not supposed to understand. Whenever they began speaking Yiddish, they would lower their voices and lean close to one another. Their warm, guttural sounds tantalized me with a world of meaning.

When we were alone, my mother would give me access to her native language. She was born in the United States to Russian immigrant parents. Yiddish was the only language she spoke until she entered kindergarten. At night she would come into my room and teach me Yiddish lullabies. Her voice, often hoarse and off-key, was nonetheless filled with the flavor of adventure. I would repeat words, phrases, whole sentences after her and then she would translate them into English. We told the story of a young Russian seamstress who could turn thread into gold, another of a young girl with a secret wish that her clever mother finally discovered and granted: a wish for a husband. Repeating the words to the songs over and over again, we made a circle of sound in the darkness. I imagined us entering that circle.

We wore colorful long skirts and high black boots. We were holding lanterns in our hands as we walked into the quiet darkness of a Russian village.

When my mother decided it was time for me to go to sleep, she would slip her arm from around my waist and kiss my forehead. I remember the soft imprint of her lips as she would say, "*Shluf, mayn feygele*" (Sleep, my little bird). "*Shluf, mayn kind*" (Sleep my child). Her love could never have been expressed quite so poignantly in English.

My father had a long-time love affair with Paris. Spending time there after World War II, he developed a particular affinity for a street named Grenelle. When he returned to New York, he discarded the name Louie Greenberg and recast himself as Louis Jerome Grennell. Marrying my mother a few years later, the Parisian street took up residence in our family as surname.

In celebration of our name and all things French, a mammoth Toulouse-Lautrec lithograph hung above our fireplace. It was a gift from my maternal grandfather. The lithograph was of a poster advertising a Parisian literary magazine called *La Revue Blanche* (The White Review). The street address was *Rue de Grenelle*. Seeing my name on a famous work of art gave me a heady sense of distinction. From my six-year-old perspective, the lady in the lithograph appeared as a giantess in a polka-dot skirt and a red-plumed hat. She was both regal and inscrutable. I was not at all sure I liked her, but I sensed she was someone to be reckoned with.

Once I began reading in English, I decided to apply my newfound skill to French. The black letters on the lithograph looked down at me challenging me to pronounce them. One day when we were standing in the living room, I asked my father to help me.

"*La Revue Blanche Bimensuelle*," I repeated after him, trying to ape his impeccable diction.

My father's laugh had a hard metallic ring. "Not like that, Steph. You're reading French, not English."

"The words are too hard," I said, defending myself both to my father and the high-toned lady in the lithograph.

The next morning my father took up the gauntlet of teaching me French. We sat on high white stools on either side of our breakfast bar facing one another. A game of colored marble balls set on wire mesh string sat between us. My counting toy, after all, had been effective in English.

"*Un, deux, trois, quatre, cinq*," my father began, pushing a ball across the string to signal the correctness of each word. His enunciation was harsh and flawless.

I cleared my throat. The marble balls glared up at me like a row of enemy soldiers.

My father nodded. "Go on."

The words stuck in my throat. "*Un, deux, trois.*"

My father put his hands over his ears in mock horror. "Not like that. Try again."

I did. Again and again and again. Each attempt was less successful than the one before it.

"If you can't speak a language perfectly, then don't speak it at all," my father said.

The world narrowed to his dark, angry face. I remember the sting of the wind in the white and yellow kitchen. The door to the back yard was ajar. We sat together in icy silence. I don't remember what happened next, but I do know that the sound of my voice in another language has brought back the shock of humiliation that I felt that day.

Stumbling Blocks

When I was seven, divorce and financial reverses took us away from the house by the sea. While my parents sculpted separate lives for themselves in Manhattan, I was sent to a boarding school in New Jersey where regimentation was the staff of life. French lessons were included in our rigorous schedule. Our French teacher, Miss Ross, smiled a lot and wore fluffy angora sweaters. She had a platinum pompadour and fat pink cheeks. Her French sounded as if she was auditioning for a part in the French-speaking version of *The Sound of Music*. She was so enamored of her voice that she rarely asked us to speak. I was grateful for that at least.

The F in French next to so many A's on my report card left my mother puzzled on Visiting Sunday. "What's going on here, Stephanie?"

"French is for nitwits," I told her.

She laughed and shook her head. Discipline was never her strong suit.

Outwardly, my father ignored this debacle. However, his despair at my ordinariness became more and more apparent at each visit. I could feel the disappointment in his long, slow steps as we walked down lawns and under grape arbors.

"You're not a smart girl, Stephanie," he said, shaking his head sadly.

The weeping willows bowed in sympathy for his bad luck. And I tried to wish my father out of existence.

When I was nine, my father devised a plan to help save me from the jaws of mediocrity. He hired a Spanish tutor. She was an older girl at my boarding school named Cheryl, who although American had lived in Argentina with her parents. She had extraordinary long legs and chestnut-colored hair. Once again I was encouraged to master the common denominator of numbers. Cheryl was never overtly critical, but her dynamism seemed to say: Why bother to try because I can do everything better than you can? I remember her swinging blithely around a tree calling out words in Spanish and asking me to repeat them. I did grudgingly, but my fledgling efforts never took wing. The lessons were soon discontinued.

My imaginative impulse to enter a world of new sounds, even as a listener, stayed dormant both in high school and college. Since I was required to study two languages, I chose Spanish and Latin. The syntax of Latin fascinated me. I loved conjugating verbs and crafting sentences. I loved deciphering the twist and curves of Caesar's escapades. What I liked best about Latin was that we didn't have to speak it.

Remaining silent in Spanish posed more of a challenge. My strength in writing and grammar won me A's. While reading aloud was usual classroom fare, conversational Spanish was rarely part of the course dynamic. In retrospect, I often think these courses might have been titled, "How Not to Learn to Speak a Language."

My father was a shadowy figure during my high school and college years. We lived separately. His criticism was so unnerving that I made every effort to avoid him. Nevertheless, I enjoyed telling people of my father's linguistic skills.

"He speaks ten languages," I would say, adding a few for good measure. I proffered his gift in compensation for my lack of one.

College came and went, and my interest in the terrain of a second language resurfaced. Casting around for new stimulation, I offered my services as a tutor in an English language learning center. There I met people from all over the world who were struggling with the hurdle of a new language and culture. I wanted to help them scale that hurdle. In time I returned to school to become a professor of English as a Second Language. The multicultural mosaic that was my classroom took me out of the tight English-thinking world that had become my frame of reference. Cultural exchange was the keynote of learning. I had the privilege of coming to understand Asian cultures. I met Russian students who knew the same stories and songs my mother had shared with me long ago.

The power of language learning also became apparent to me. I learned that English could provide a springboard for students to discover new parts of themselves. An Israeli student in her early twenties wrote me a letter explaining that the imaginative quality of her spoken and written voice in English amazed her; she had experienced herself as dry and matter-of-fact in Hebrew. I had admiration for her courage. The journey into an unknown world of sound was still my nemesis.

My father was fearful about my new career.

The specter of his criticism was still apparent. "How can you teach people English when you don't know their language?" he quizzed me.

Toward the end of his life my father often reminisced about his years at Harvard, depicting himself as a young man walking the breadth of the college campus. These had been the best years of his life, he said. It was at Harvard that he had written a senior thesis that won him first prize and the promise of a doctoral scholarship to Oxford in languages and philosophy. After graduating, my father discarded the world of academia for a career in business. His yearning, however, for the life he might have led was never extinguished. He died on a rainy October day in 1988. At his funeral, his wife and I made certain that the rabbi commemorated his gift for languages in his eulogy.

Silent Journeys

The summer after my father's death, I visited the Harvard campus. I walked the tree-lined pathways that had been the hub of his intellectual life. In the Harvard library, I discovered his senior thesis. Only the prize-winning documents remained on the shelves. My hand shook with excitement as I opened the cover. In 40 well-substantiated pages, my father explained how *The Celestina*, a dramatic dialogue written in 15th-century Spain, had influenced 200 years of world literature. Some of the text was written in Spanish. I could feel my father's life force coursing through those pages. This was not the voice of a man who would have dashed his own hopes or the hopes of his children.

The following summer I traveled to Spain. The sun-bleached houses of the Costa Brava mesmerized me with their beauty. In Barcelona, Gaudi's architecture, mimicking the shapes and textures of trees, spoke to me of Spain's individual spirit. I was determined to speak out loud, if only to order a meal in a restaurant. My nerve failed me. I relied on my traveling companion's acumen for languages.

My love for the sound of the Spanish language was revived on that trip. A few months later a friend went to Paris to do research on a book synthesizing 19th-century impressionist painting and picnic recipes. She asked me to spend some time with her Spanish-speaking fiancé while she was away. He was a congenial dentist from Santiago named Julio who spoke clear, precise Spanish and only a smidgen of English. We spent a long afternoon together viewing paintings at the Museum of Modern Art. Standing in front of a Cezanne still life, our conversation took on the lucidity of the painting. Julio spoke in Spanish, and I spoke in English. We understood each other perfectly. My excitement mounted as I realized I could attribute meaning to his sounds. That this conversation was taking place in a public space was all the more thrilling. It was a matter of record. If not yet a Spanish speaker, I had become a competent listener.

On my next vacation, I went to Italy. I had the privilege of viewing the Bay of Naples, the ebullient flowers of Tuscany, the pristine mission of Monte Cassino high above the city, the splendor of the Vatican, the Tower of Pisa. At night I would hear myself speaking the Italian language in my dreams, passion and pathos ringing in every syllable. By day, however, tour guides and a Rumanian friend, who was a fearless language learner, did my speaking for me. The prospect of hearing my own voice in another language still filled me with angst.

Finding my way to Paris in the spring of 1994, I stayed in a small hotel on the *Rue de Grenelle*, the street from which my father had taken his name. The City of Lights pulled on my every nerve with its radiance. Getting around and speaking to people was another matter. I discovered the French were not very tolerant of my only-English mentality. I paced back and forth in my hotel room, a vise of fear working its way around my neck. How could I negotiate a meal or the Metro without speaking French? Forcing myself outside into the cool March air, I paced up and down the *Rue de Grenelle*, studying the open fruit markets and the delicate iron latticework on the buildings. Gingerly I entered a boulangerie. I could not bring myself to say, "*Croissant, s'il vous plait.*" Instead I pointed to a plump croissant that looked especially delicious. The woman behind the counter gave me the sad-looking roll next to it instead. With a flush of embarrassment, I took the roll, paid, and bounded for the street. I entered a supermarket determined to buy fruit; an alarm bell sounded because I had mistaken the exit for the entrance. Dizzy with shame, I left without making a purchase. I found ways to circumvent the language. I visited the Louvre and the Rodin Museum, knowing the guards would speak to me in English. I took an English-speaking bus tour around the city.

The city was alive with light the day I left Paris. I walked up and down the *Rue de Grenelle* taking pictures of the apothecary, the *patisserie*, the *Grenelle Immobilier*, and a small park with a waterfall enlivened by sunshine. My senses were completely attuned to the moment. I wanted to record, memorize, and extend my experience. A car lurched unexpectedly, causing a stylish woman in a black cape and myself to jump back. There was a touch of irony and familiarity in our smiles when we knew we were safe. She did not regard me as a foreigner.

I felt a sense of anticipation entering the *boulangerie* for my final breakfast.

"*Croissant, s'il vous plaît,*" I said softly.

A smile played on the woman's lips as she handed me the croissant.

"*Merci beaucoup*," I said with more certainty.

"*Merci à vous, madame*," she replied.

I felt a remarkable lightness as I walked out into the sunshine.

The taxi driver was in a jovial mood on our way to the airport. "*Très jolie*," he said, waving expansively at his city.

"*Très jolie*," I agreed enthusiastically.

His French, while magnificent in cadence, was incomprehensible to me.

I explained in a clear audible voice, "*Je ne parle pas français. Parlez-vous anglais?*"

"*Oui, un peu*," he said. "First time in Paris?"

He turned to look at me. I remember his shaggy black hair and bright smile. I nodded.

"Come back again?"

"*Oui*," I said.

"*Bon*. Next time you speak French."

Part IV

OUR LOVE AFFAIRS WITH LANGUAGES: STORIES OF MULTI-LANGUAGE LEARNERS

The meditations written by the four polyglots in this section reveal language learning as a way of getting outside of oneself. According to these authors, language learning could help one to overcome a certain kind of insularity or claustrophobia. Feelings of play, spontaneity, and exploration are described. Language learning for these writers provides opportunities to transcend the self, to develop new ideas, to experience different emotions. The experience is often likened to having a love affair. For these writers, however, the lovers are words.

The opening piece, written by Watson Millison, pays tribute to his parents for providing him with a trilingual childhood (he is the son of Doug Millison, whose chapter appears in the next section). He describes how speaking different languages to his parents in his bilingual/bicultural home gives him a way to bond with and get closer to them, by sharing their culture and experiences as language learners.

George Jochnowitz writes from the perspective of a linguist who has always loved languages, and learned many of them throughout his life. Discussing language learning both in classrooms and in natural environments, his piece combines intellectual insights with personal experiences to shed light on the process of consciously learning foreign languages, as opposed to acquiring them naturally through immersion (see Krashen, 1981). Interestingly, the end of his piece, like Stephanie Hart's in the previous section, takes place in a taxicab. As a New Yorker, I can appreciate this, knowing as I do the taxi as an ubiquitous location for some of the most profound and urgent multi-cultural, multiracial, and multilingual discourse exchanges.

Christina Kotchemidova's piece underscores the theme that language, like love, allows one to transcend the self, to experience other perspectives and ways of being:

Speaking a foreign language I am a mechanic with a special instrument, a person of status, a conqueror, a master, a person with a hobby, a sportsperson, a structuralist, a mason, an artist, a philosopher, a hedonist, a scholar, a priest, an actor . . . in love and . . . young . . . a multiple personality . . . a goddess!

Cora Acebron Tolosa, also known as *un monumento a la capacidad lingüística*, considers in her piece what has drawn her so powerfully to some languages and distanced her from others. In her passionately told piece, she introduces us to her entourage of "friends and acquaintances" (languages) she has had intimate relationships with throughout the years.

Reference

Krashen, S. (1981). *Second language acquisition and second language learning*. Oxford: Pergamon.

18

Me, Times Three:
Growing Up Trilingual

WATSON R. MILLISON

Growing up trilingual isn't easy. It is hard to learn two other languages that are totally different from English. But knowing three languages also makes my life a lot richer.

My mother is Chinese. She was born and raised in the People's Republic of China. She grew up speaking standard Chinese, *putong hua*, also known as Mandarin dialect. She can speak Shanghai dialect, and she understands Hangzhou dialect. Her parents speak *putong hua*, Shanghai dialect, plus their local dialects. *Ah Gong* ("grandfather" in Shanghainese) speaks *Jiashan* dialect. *Ah Bu* ("grandmother") speaks *Wuxi* dialect. They both know Hangzhou dialect, too. These dialects are native to the southeastern part of China, near Shanghai. They sound very different from *putong hua*, like completely different languages.

Mom came to the United States in 1980 and met my father in Berkeley, California. My father is American. His native language is English, but he speaks fluent French and pretty good Chinese. I came into the world in Santa Ana, California, in 1987. My mom and I were staying at my Uncle Sam's house. Uncle Sam is my mother's little brother. My dad was in China, finishing up a Chinese-language study program. I was surrounded by Chinese-speaking people from my first moments: my mother, my uncle, my aunt, and my maternal grandmother, who came from Beijing. The only English-speaking person in the house was my paternal grandmother, who came from Texas to help because my dad was in Beijing.

My dad came back to California when I was three months old. I don't remember it, but he tells me that he used to take me outside on the patio and show me things, pronouncing the name of each object in English: *bird*, *tree*, *flower*, *sky*, *house*, *sun*, *moon*, *stars*. I couldn't talk back, of course.

I started talking when I was about 18 months old. By then my family had moved to Santa Clara, California. Ah Gong and Ah Bu had immigrated from China and they lived with us and took care of me while Mom and Dad went to work. The very first words I spoke were Chinese: I learned to say *Ah Bu*, then *Ah Gong*. Soon after that, I began speaking English with my dad.

I continued speaking English and Chinese for the next couple of years. I went to a family day care center run by a Chinese lady. I was also learning more English from my dad, from television, and from people in the city around me. I spoke both languages all the time. Sometimes I mixed them up, even in the same sentence.

When I was four years old, I started going to the East Bay French-American School in Berkeley, also called *École Bilingue de Berkeley*. EB is a bilingual school. The students learn all their subjects in French and in English. We follow the same curriculum as schools in France, plus a lot of study in English. In prekindergarten and kindergarten, we were immersed in French. Starting in first grade, the program was about 70% in French, 30% in English. Over the years, the time spent in English-language instruction gradually increased to about half and half now that I'm in the sixth grade (*6ième* in the French system).

I didn't know any French when I started at EB. All the kids were new, too. It was a strange experience. I learned the names of all the objects in the classroom. We learned how to sing French songs and play French games. But there were a lot of things I didn't know how to say or ask.

In first grade, I learned how to read and write in French. I could already read in English. My dad used to read to me in English, and I gradually picked it up while he was reading to me. My dad tells me how surprised he was one day when he was reading me *The Hobbit*, a novel by J. R. R. Tolkien. He turned the page, but before he could resume, I continued reading at the top of the next page. I was five years old. I had also learned to write English at day care, and in pre-K and kindergarten at EB. Learning to read and write in French felt very different: I had to use more energy and time as I was talking, and sometimes I would stumble over certain words that I knew in English, but not in French. Learning how to speak French felt like trying to pronounce the words with marbles in my mouth. But with the help of my teacher, Collette, I was soon making progress in reading and writing French.

When I started kindergarten at EB, Mom started sending me to Chinese school on Saturday mornings. I learned how to say hello and say the other things I needed to know in order to deal with the teacher and the class. I started learning how to read and write Chinese, first in *Pinyin*, a simplified phonetic system, then in standard Chinese characters, *hanzi*. At first it felt really different, but as I learned more characters and vocabulary it became easier. What I liked most about Chinese school was that we earned points for doing our homework. At the end of each month, we could exchange points for prizes. I liked learning Chinese at this school enough to attend through fifth grade. After fifth grade, Mom wasn't happy with the curriculum, so we hired our own Chinese teacher to tutor me and a couple of Chinese friends on Saturdays. Now I read and write Chinese at about a third grade level, and my conversational skills are good enough to let me communicate easily in Chinese with my family.

I feel the most comfortable in English. It's easy. Words just come to me in a snap. I speak more quickly, too. If I'm lazy and don't want to take the time to speak in French or Chinese, I use English. English is the language I use with my friends when I'm having fun. It's the language I use to enjoy television and the newspaper sports page.

Chinese is the language I use with my mom, her parents, and my other Chinese relatives. It's more difficult to communicate, but I know they feel closer to me when I use Chinese with them. Chinese can also be fun, especially when I cuddle up on the couch with Mom and watch a funny Chinese TV show. My Chinese vocabulary is still relatively small, but with my mom and grandparents, I can mix Chinese and English and they can usually understand.

For me, French is a language I use to learn at school, in my academic experience. Sometimes I speak French with my dad, when he helps me with my homework. When my homework assignments are hard, it's a struggle. Getting some insight from my teachers or my dad lets me do my work more efficiently. After understanding the assignment and learning something new in French, I feel as if my brain has connected to another world.

What I'm trying to accomplish is to be able to speak, read, and write equally well in English, Chinese, and French. I am working hard to achieve this goal.

Being trilingual lets me know my family better, gives me more chances to make friends around the world, gives me a greater variety of books and movies and television shows, and lets me enjoy myself more when I travel.

I've had a chance to travel to France and China twice. I went to China the first time when I was four, with Mom. We stayed at my aunt's apartment at the Beijing University of Aeronautics and Astronautics. I had a chance to visit lots of nearby attractions like the Great Wall. My Chinese improved a lot. I went again the summer after fourth grade. Mom took me to Beijing and Xian, then I stayed for another month with my aunt and cousin in Beijing. I had a chance to participate in a special day of activities for overseas Chinese people to celebrate learning Chinese. My picture was in the *People's Daily* newspaper, I was on the national television news, and I was a guest on a talk show. It was very exciting.

I went to France with my mom and dad the summer before first grade. We stayed with my parents' friends in Paris. I was able to talk and play with their two boys, who are about my age, and I could talk with people we met as we toured the city and ate in restaurants. Dad says the Parisians thought I was a very clever boy. I went back to France again near the end of fifth grade, on a two-week school exchange program. Being fluent in French made it easy to talk with my host family and the people I met while I was there. I started feeling more and more French, but at the same time I didn't forget I was American and Chinese.

Being trilingual has given me many great experiences, but it causes some problems, too. The biggest problem is not having as much time to play because I have to spend so much time studying. I would have much more free time if all I had to worry about was English. However, this is the way I've grown up. I don't really know another way. Even my name reflects my heritage. My English name is Watson Richard Millison. Richard was my dad's maternal grandfather's name. Watson comes from my Chinese name, which *Ah Gong* selected for me: *Mi Hua Sun*. *Mi* is short for Millison. *Hua* is *Ah Bu's* family name and it also means China. *Sun* is *Ah Gong's* family name, my mom's family name. If you say *Mi Hua Sun* quickly, it sounds a little like Millison, too. I guess having a French name would be just too complicated. The way you pronounce my name in French is: Watsòn Milli-sòn.

Growing up trilingual means me being me, times three.

19

My Love Affair with Languages

GEORGE JOCHNOWITZ

I have always loved languages. I want to speak them and to know how they work. That is why I studied linguistics.

My mother told me that I was bilingual in Yiddish and English until I started kindergarten at the age of five. I don't think I could have been. My maternal grandparents, who lived about a 15–minute walk from our apartment in the Borough Park section of Brooklyn, had come to America when they were middle-aged. They spoke Yiddish to me; my parents spoke Yiddish to them even though they used only English at home. All the same, as far back as I can remember—I know that the memories of being a three- or four- or five-year-old child are few and far between—I always thought in English. When I spoke Yiddish, I was conscious of trying to find the right words. It was an effort, even though my pronunciation was perfect. The same is true today.

My pronunciation has often misled people. I speak Chinese badly and Polish almost not at all. Yet when I say a few words, I pronounce them well. Listeners think I can really communicate in Polish or Chinese and are mystified when I don't understand what they are saying. I suspect that even my own mother did not realize how inadequate my childhood command of Yiddish was.

Hebrew was the first foreign language I studied formally, starting at age 7. A friend of my grandfather's came to the house every Wednesday, and I took lessons in saying the prayers and reading the Bible. We never quite made it through Genesis. There was a missing element in my instruction: conversation. Learning vocabulary and grammar is both pleasurable and useful, but practice in the spoken language is needed as well. Although Biblical Hebrew is closer to the spoken language of Israel than Chaucer's language (and maybe even Shakespeare's) is to ours, no one quite speaks the ancient language. Theory and practice are both essential to language learning, except for a child, who can pick up languages through mere exposure.

My study of Hebrew led to an unexpected fringe benefit: I learned to read Yiddish. If you can read one language and speak another, you can learn to read the second without much effort. If a new alphabet is involved, learning it is a minor problem. Having been taught Hebrew letters, I could read Yiddish as soon as the rules relating the writing system to the sound system were explained to me. I suspect that a great many Yiddish speakers were never taught to read Yiddish but simply figured it out after they took a few Hebrew lessons.

Alphabets are very easy and logical. English spelling is somewhat unpredictable in terms of sounds. When I was about seven years old, I decided to remedy this flaw by devising a new way to write English based entirely on pronunciation. I abandoned my project after a while when I saw that nobody wanted it. But when I reached the age of 13, I found something in my junior high school textbook that renewed my confidence in the value of what had been my fantasy as a seven-year-old.

The textbook in question was called *Parlez-vous français?* It used strange characters within brackets to indicate the pronunciation of each word. My teachers ignored them. These funny symbols were the International Phonetic Alphabet (IPA), and they were explained in the appendix at the end of the book. Reading the appendix showed me that I was not the first person to invent a phonetic alphabet. My idle thoughts about sounds had not been so idle after all. I read about "high front rounded vowels" and learned how to pronounce the French *u*. My French teacher was dazzled. Years later, when I reached graduate school and studied phonetics, I rediscovered IPA, an old friend.

In high school, my friend Jimmy Brown and I learned to love opera. When we were 15, we went to a performance of *The Marriage of Figaro* at the Amato Opera Theater, which used to be located on Bleecker Street. The performance was in English, and neither of us knew the story. All the surprises worked for us; we saw the opera as it was meant to be seen.

I bought a recording of the opera, in Italian, of course. I listened to it every day for a year. The following year, my daily listening was *Cavalleria Rusticana*. I followed the *libretto* enclosed in the album: Italian on one side, English on the other. Italian is extremely similar to French. In college, I went to the head of the Italian Department and told him that I had never studied Italian, but that I probably could enter the second-semester course. He gave me a grammar book and told me to come back in two weeks. We spoke in Italian for a few minutes before he placed me in a second-year class.

Let me skip over some 20-odd years. I was 46, and I had been invited to teach at Hebei University in Baoding, China. I took a six-week intensive summer course in Mandarin Chinese before I left New York. I wondered whether I would be able to learn the difference between *ma* on a high tone, meaning "Mommy," and *ma* on a low, falling-rising tone, meaning "horse." I found that I could learn to say the tones easily, but I had to be told which tone I was hearing, at least for a while. The tones turned out to be a minor problem. The fact that relative clauses precede the nouns they modify was a slightly bigger problem; by the time I realized that there was a relative clause in the sentence, the speaker had gone on and I was lost.

Living in China should have made it easy for me to pick up new vocabulary, but it was harder than I had ever expected. The problem was that I could never really learn to read. There are just too many Chinese characters, and I was just too hooked on alphabets. If you can read, you see a new word one day and hear it the next. Reading and speaking always reinforce each other. Reading Chinese is just plain hard. It's even hard for Chinese children, who don't learn to read as quickly as children whose language is written in an alphabet. Besides, I was in my forties. Although I could learn grammar and pronunciation as quickly as ever, I had no experience in learning to read ideograms. As you get older, the things you have learned how to learn can be acquired with greater and greater ease. The things you haven't learned how to learn, on the other hand, are quite hard to crack.

Grammars don't frighten me. When I took Chinese in class, I learned as well as when I had started French at the age of 12, if not better. When I lived in China, however, I came across grammatical constructions I couldn't figure out. There was a past tense formed by adding *le* and another formed by adding *de*. Whenever someone corrected me, I asked why. "It doesn't sound good," I was told. They both sounded equally good and equally Chinese to me. What I needed was someone who could express the rules verbally in addition to knowing them instinctively. I couldn't get an answer until I got back to the United States, where I was able to find a teacher who was experienced in teaching Chinese to Americans. She was able to tell me that *le* was used to establish past time, after which *de* was used to discuss time or place in the past. I couldn't figure it out for myself because it hadn't occurred to me that a language needed to make a distinction of this sort between two different past tenses.

Adults have to be taught grammar. You can guess the rule if you are acquiring a closely related language, as I could when I learned Italian. It is much more difficult, however, to generalize about grammatical categories that don't exist in your own language. We adults are already in the habit of thinking in our own languages. Explaining a rule is simple and comprehensible; figuring it out is impossible, unless you have been presented with contrasting sets of sentences. In that case, of course, the selection of examples is in itself an explanation.

Distinctions must be pointed out to those learning a new language. This is true for both grammar and sounds. Just as I didn't know to expect an extra Chinese past tense, Spanish students and Chinese students don't now that they should listen for the difference in the vowels of *fit* and *feet*. Their ears are just as good as those of English speakers, but they have not learned to pay attention to this difference. Similarly, English speakers do not expect a change in the pitch to mean that an entirely different word has been said. To cite my previous example, when you say *ma* on a high tone it means "mommy"; on a low falling-rising tone it means "horse."

Hearing and using a language are essential. So is theoretical knowledge. Using a single approach is not enough when dealing with a structure as immense and as complicated as a language.

Explaining a rule is very simple if you have learned just what the rule is. Discovering a rule, even if it is a rule you use every day, is much more difficult. Discovering a rule in a language you hardly know is next to impossible, especially if the rule refers to a distinction you had never imagined. How many English speakers can explain what is wrong with "I have eaten breakfast at 7:15 this morning," or why you can't say "The truck delivered 14 furnitures"? (The answers are that a present perfect tense like "have eaten" can never be used with an expression of definite time, and that "furniture" is not a member of the class of countable nouns in English.) Children can make these generalizations; adults can't. Practice doesn't help if you practice mistakes.

Chinese was not the last language I studied. I went to visit Poland in 1990 and took six Polish lessons before my trip. They turned out to be surprisingly useful, not only in Poland but in New York. I would like to end this memoir with an account of a taxi ride:

I got into the cab and said "First Avenue and 62nd Street."

The driver, Wlodzimierz, turned to me saying, "No speak."

We were heading east, and he drove straight ahead, showing no sign of turning left at First Avenue.

"*W lewo*" (to the left), I said.

He turned left and proceeded up First Avenue.

"You Jew?" he inquired politely.

I said, "Yes."

After arriving at my destination and paying him, I said, "*Do widzenia*" (goodbye).

"*Shalom*," he answered.

20

Looking for the God of Language

CHRISTINA KOTCHEMIDOVA

Within the Pantheon of gods on Olympia, one god is missing: I have always wondered why the ancient Greeks didn't have a god of language. Did they feel that language—unlike love, nature, and the arts—is a human invention, nothing more than a tool to work with?

Knowing a foreign language is a bit like having an extra instrument or one more piece of software to use. I can produce intellectual products for a second market, and I benefit from exploring that market in terms of the ideas it offers. I am privileged. I have two accesses to human mental achievement while most of my confrères have only one. I feel knowledgeable, a person of greater opportunities. In a way, I am superior, and everybody is ready to recognize it. My expertise in a foreign language has subtly won me status.

A foreign language is a mind-opener. It breaks up my habitual horizon to introduce me into a world of different culture and sensibility. Coming to know this world, I am appropriating it—so here I am, a conqueror of new mental territories.

Learning a language, of course, is a lot of hard work. But most of us realize that to get satisfaction, one must first invest an effort, and the greater the effort, the more fun later. So we undertake the hardships of learning a language with the expectations of being rewarded. In this respect, a foreign language is very much like a hobby—something situated between work and pleasure—an occupation you are willing to spend time on because it makes you happy.

Like learning a sport, language takes you through all the stages between walking on crutches and graceful dancing. Trying to come up with the right phrase is like running hurdles. Every hurdle overcome makes me proud of myself. I become a heroine in my own eyes. Speaking a non-native language, I am taking risks at every moment: Will I measure up to the standards, or will I make a fool of myself?

A tickling sense of insecurity keeps me on the alert all the time. Oscillating between prospects of success and failure, I've had my tonic for the day—without it, life would be too monotonous.

Studying grammar makes me think about patterns. I realize I am filling existing structures with elements, and it starts dawning on me that the whole world might be about structure. I don't have to go into the science of linguistics to find out that structuralism makes sense. I can feel the relevance of structure as I play with words, morphemes, parts of the sentence. Thrown in at random, they don't mean a thing. But used by the rules of grammar, they make up constructions as fascinating as a Lego game. I am building castles, cosy little huts, or giant skyscrapers. I am a mason.

Trying to phrase my thoughts in a non-native language, I am focusing on form, or at least, I am constantly aware of the relationship between form and content, since the substance is well-known to me but I am experimenting just by giving it a new form. No matter how trivial the conversation, I am as formalistic as I can only be if I am working in the arts. Pronouncing the exact sounds, weaving the right phrase, provides me with a sense of perfection. I experience the aesthetic pleasure of being in tune with many others, thus forming an orchestra.

Learning a language makes me a child again.

I blunder all the time and the others seem to excuse it.

There is so much to discover. Translated, the world around me looks unfamiliar. Just describing it for my homework makes me open my eyes for it anew. As rigid as my ideas about reality might be, the very process of projecting them into a different formal system is changing them. I may very well have known all my life that I am "my mother's daughter," but learning that I am *"la fille de ma mère"* is amusing. Repeating basic truths makes me giggle secretly. Didn't Eugene Ionesco get his idea for the theater of the absurd from a language textbook where he learned that his father was his mother's husband while his mother was his father's wife?

Switching into a foreign language, I feel playful. I am a kid who has suddenly been given a new set of toys to replace the old one she was bored with. Every object around me has been renamed. I develop a fresh interest in it. Is it really the same? What kind of game is this?

I once tutored a mentally ill Bulgarian man who wanted to learn English just because he was fascinated by the fact that the same thing could be said in two totally different ways. "Which is true?" he kept asking until my whole idea of reality was shattered. I actually found out that a foreign language makes you *think* in a different way, since it carries a specific perception of reality inherent in it. For example, in English we say, "What is your

name?," the presumption being that you *have* a name, you are in posses-
sion of a name that is your own, and therefore you are very much in control of your own identity. In Russian the expression is, *"Kak tebia zavout?"*
[How do people call you?], implying that you are a passive object that has
been *given* a name by others. In French, *"Comment t'appelles-tu?"* has always
struck me as rather narcissistic, as if I'm constantly *calling myself* and am
therefore constantly preoccupied with myself.

So, just like my mentally ill student, I ask myself: Which is true? Which
one expresses the actual relationship between myself and my name? And,
subsequently, what *is* that relationship, anyway?

I have the urge to undertake scholarly research on the subject, and
before I know it, I've turned into a philosopher! Soon I start realizing that
language has nothing to do with reality. It is not a reflection/mirror/pro-
jection of reality in any way. It is rather a meta-reality where objects and
ideas are very inaccurately reproduced, just roughly molded into concepts
and images, making up a world of abstraction. Language, then, becomes a
spiritual experience I am initiated into. Especially when translating, I
become constantly aware of this ideal realm I have to go through every
time I'm looking for an equivalent. I move among absolutes, reveling in
their purity, then try to nail them down into imperfect earthly shapes. I
am a priest bringing down heavenly truths to a congregation of sheep.

Like religion—from Latin *religare*, to link—language unites you with
other people. You become part of the big family speaking a certain language. Having more family, in turn, makes you feel less solitary and vul-
nerable on earth. Thus, knowing foreign languages reduces one's metaphysical fears. That's one reason why it is revitalizing.

Speaking a foreign language is very much like being in love.

I am striving for communication, which, in its essence, is a kind of
unification with another person. Once achieved, it fills me with joy. At every
brisk moment of understanding I hear bells ringing. Gradually, I come to
know my partner's mind—and isn't that, fundamentally, an act of love?

The world looks as new and interesting in a foreign language as it does
to happy youngsters in love.

I am implicitly asking my interlocutor for more than the standard dose
of attention (just to be properly understood) and eventually I get it, very
much as in a love relationship.

I am constantly testing ground with my partner. I am stepping back
and forth between what is banally accepted and what is courageously
invented on the spot. I am flirting—inviting my partner to venture into
understanding me just as I am venturing into his/her home territory.

Finally, speaking a foreign language is erotic in terms of my own persona. Tuning into another language, I undergo a transformation as if I am

performing. Saying "hello" in Japanese requires a bow, and here I am, humble and obedient as I would never be in English. Speaking Russian, I tend to use diminutives because they are typical of the culture and somehow expected in the language. I suppose this makes me look more emotional and sentimental than I normally am. Am I misrepresenting myself? Surprisingly enough, I *do* feel somewhat emotional and sentimental when I'm speaking Russian. The very language I am using has changed me.

Language is so pregnant with culture—habits, moral values, attitudes—that I find myself acquiring a different cultural identity in every language that I speak. Just asking about the train to the capital—in England I have to talk about the *nonstop train*, a strong understatement for a train that beats all others, here being characterized by the minor fact that it does not stop at intermediate points. In French I find myself talking about the *train direct*, drawing a straight line in my mind, while in Italian I am asking about the *express*—implicitly admiring this unsurpassable and very special train indeed.

The point is, just using the appropriate words, I look reserved in English, rational in French, affected in Italian, as the respective cultures require. I am putting on different faces.

And I seem to be doing this in order to be accepted, to be liked. As in a desperate love relationship, I am trying to please the partner I am with to the point of not being myself.

In Bulgarian the protocol of communication is very much like a ritual. Being to the point and businesslike would seem, on most occasions, rude or ill-mannered. Among Americans, conversely, baroque phrases of introduction seem completely silly. Am I the same person doing both?

Changing one's cultural identity is quite stimulating. One can easily be overwhelmed with one's own self. This is especially energizing if you're bored with yourself to death. I sometimes become narcissistic to the point of mistaking any nod of understanding on the part of my interlocutor for an approval of my own persona.

So, speaking a foreign language, I am a mechanic with a special instrument, a person of status, a conqueror, a master, a person with a hobby, a sportsperson, a structuralist, a mason, an artist, a philosopher, a hedonist, a scholar, a priest, an actor. I am in love and I am young. I am a multiple personality. I am a goddess! Language is the one thing that can place humans anywhere near the gods. It makes all of us constantly produce something as bizarre and imperfect and fascinating in its imperfection as creation itself. Like creation, language is the product of a genius mind, only that of a collective genius—so isn't it all the more admirable since so many individuals have worked together on the same gigantic project?

No wonder the ancient Greeks didn't need a god of language. The place is taken by the human race.

21

Why I Never Lost My Accent

CORA ACEBRÓN TOLOSA

My friend Tere usually introduces me to her friends by saying, "and this is Cora Acebrón, a monument to linguistic capacity," and proceeds without pause to list the languages that I more or less speak and a few others that she adds out of friendly overzealousness. The first time that I heard Tere's flamboyant expression, "*un monumento a la capacidad lingüística*," I saw myself turned into rock and placed in some minor square of Cuenca, my hometown in Spain, or in one of the little alcoves in the park that house the statues of the local luminaries. The fear of such metamorphosis always rushed me into apologies for Tere's hyperbolic misrepresentation. I remember flushing years ago as I hurried to explain with clumsiness, in case anybody had taken Tere seriously, that Roman Jakobson, who knew over 200 languages, was a monument to all sorts of capacities; that I just "coped" somehow as any other educated young European would. My confusion sounded sometimes a bit arrogant, and I just made everything worse. Today my fear of petrification has gone, but I still feel awkward in the Spain of the EEC when Tere revisits the monument theme.

When I began thinking about this piece, I confessed to my friend Susan that I could not understand why I had been able to learn certain languages and was so incapable of even bearing the idea of learning others. Susan said, "Well, dearie"—she calls me "dearie"—"it seems that all you do, you do it for love; so think about it." Now, Susan is a saint, and her remark was just typical of her blessedness. But I trust her a lot, and decided to explore her angle, which is really not far from the target at all.

I do not know how I acquired the taste for words, or how I learned to enjoy the different nuances of different sounds. It might have been my grandfather Tino's singing or praying in Euskera, the ancient tongue of the

Basques in Spain; or it might have been my father's splendid voice coming through the radio waves in those literary commentaries of my distant childhood; or my mother's velvety soprano quality, inherited from her mother, who was not allowed to study voice because it was not a decent thing to do for a decent woman those days. Fate, perhaps, is what it was.

I have studied many languages. I have become familiar with some, good friends with others, and I have totally sent to oblivion a good handful. I praised one of my brothers recently because of his ability to make lots of friends all the time, and I told him how much I regretted having lost so many of my friends after so many changes of residence. He reminded me that there are acquaintances, and then there are friends; and that acquaintances are many and they come and go, and friends are few and most of them remain forever. About languages I could say what my brother says about people.

I revisit my German with pain each time I need to read an article, because I never quite acquired a taste for it. I have traveled in Germany and I have always enjoyed the country and the detached politeness of the Germans, but I always stepped to a second line there, so that my lover could charm everyone with her limited but polished German. For years I tried to make Rilke my motivation to learn, but I had fallen captive to Rilke in Spanish when I was barely 16, and I found delight in memorizing parts of *The Notebook of Malte Laurids Brigge* and a few of the *Duino Elegies*. Not even today, with my supposed maturity and scholarly abilities, can I bring myself to read Rilke in German.

I studied Old Slavonic for two years, and only recently gave away the magazines (nostalgia can be so cluttering) that the University of Sofia sent me regularly many years after I had ceased caring for the teachings of Saint Cyril. It was not the thrill of a different alphabet, since I had been studying Greek for years already. I could not seriously say that I wanted to know the language in which so many beautiful pieces of the Orthodox liturgical music had been written, so I justified to myself that digression from my studies in Classics by explaining that I needed Old Slavonic for my work in Indoeuropean. I occupied myself then with "the history of the u," as one of my professors mockingly called it. Today I find it hard to believe that I had the patience to write my master's thesis on Indoeuropean vocabulary. The truth is that I moved on and had no use for Old Slavonic. I still adore, however, the music of the Orthodox Church.

Something similar happened with my fling at classical Arabic. I had read and loved the medieval Hispano-Arabic poets Ben Sahl, Ar-Rusafi, and Ben Hazm. The intense eroticism of their verses filled my senses with desire and fragrances of quinces, wine, and jasmine. I found delight very early in my adolescent years in energizing my Spanish with words of Arabic descent. My mouth tasted mint and spices when I could brighten my speech with *alhucema, aljófar, ajonjolí* (lavender, pearl, sesame). But the truth is that I studied Arabic in college because I was tired of Greek. During those two years I was truly happy. It was a sensuous language, and very flexible and liberating after the atrocities of Greek grammar. I almost changed majors. I even liked the department better: it was mostly women, very friendly and helpful, dressed very casually, and with none of the snub noses that populated, nay, overcrowded, the Classics department. But, forced to choose forever between Latin and Arabic, I gave up the passion of Ben Sahl and returned to Classics.

My attempts at Arabic, at Slavonic, and even at German were never too serious, and I do not have a feeling of loss or failure for not knowing the languages. I had fun with them and then, as my brother would say, I moved to another country. But my relationship with Greek—now I am getting into deeper levels of acquaintance—undermines Tere's flattery and supports Susan's intuition.

I hate Greek. I really do. I have suffered so much with it that I do not even care anymore about Plato or Aristophanes. Not even about Sappho. And I thoroughly dislike Euripides. And it is because all Hellenists I have known wear this highfalutin' cape of perverse arrogance that seems to have been cut by the same tailor. Here is where I can be labeled an ignoramus; here is where my ex-lover would remind me of the need to be "rational" in life; here is where any self-respecting classicist would see my reputation and future tarnished and polluted forever.

But here is where I recall my discomfort—oh, how kind I am—with *doña* Gloria Sedeño, my boring and aloof Greek teacher in high school. Here is where I recall *don* Luis Gil in my third year of college Greek, with his thick, wild gray eyebrows peeping over his little rectangular reading glasses, staunchly fixed on his nose, like buttresses on a wall. I recall his rhetorical mastery, more impressive than most because he never raised his voice and could perorate for an hour with exquisite dactylic regularity. *Don* Luis was a modern sophist, and fashioned himself after those ancient virtuosi of the word: Fond of speech more as a sport than as a pedagogical tool, he was peevish, cruel, and delicious reading Lucian and Herodotus and advising a large number of my classmates—me, alas, included—to give up the study of the language of Homer and go to "one of those American universities" where, instead, we could take bongo-playing classes. Here is where I recall Professor Adrados, who taught me Greek syntax, and who used to guide us through the Archaeological Museum repeating in his peculiar stutter, "It's Roman, don't look." Here is where I recall Professor Ruipérez, who taught me Greek phonetics, and who used to throw the eraser to the floor after he cleaned the blackboard so that he could bend down and pick it up and, while exercising his waist, have a good look at the girls' legs under the desks. And here too is where I recall the famous professor in New York, famous for her ruses, her fur coats, her high heels in snowstorms, her wandering eye, her ultra-pyrenaic demeanor, her dismissive abruptness, and her classes, so tedious, interminable, and soporiferous that more than once nobody registered to take them.

I learned Greek unhappily and poorly, because I never loved who taught it. I should end here the account of my relationship with dead languages, but I must break my climax to recall my love for my Latin teachers. I really loved *don* Juan José in high school. I still do. I feel a warmth each time I visit him that is all joy and pleasure, but I don't quite know how to tell him how much of my happiness I owe to him and his teachings. He was exquisite and erudite, but his erudition was always softened with a humbleness that put everybody at ease. He had class, he had style, and he had a tenderness with the students that I have never seen matched. He taught me how to read Latin, not how to translate it. He taught me how to enjoy the pure sound of the words, and how to enjoy making that sound myself. With him I fell in love with Dido's passion and Hannibal's complexities; and with him I learned how to enjoy Livy's storytelling, and his quaint and enthusiastic patriotism.

Don Juan José embodied the totality of perfection that no other teacher has ever equaled, but after him I still was very lucky with my Latin teachers. I recall Professor Otón Sobrino, that little, quiet man, who taught me to read not Virgil, but myself in Virgil. I recall Professor Augustín García Calvo, in platform shoes and silk scarves, who taught me that meaning, and sound, and rhythm are all one; who never wasted our energies making us work for the sake of a grade; and who might be the best educated man in the entire globe, and perhaps the one with the prettiest voice. And I recall Professor Alan Cameron, always kind, funny, patient, and supportive even when there is not much to support.

I never really learned Greek, never made it part of me, because all those eminent Hellenists always made me feel a prisoner of the language, of its irregularities, of its rules, of its particles, of its sacrosanct untouchability. Latin is part of me because those Latinists opened the world with me, and I plunged into it freely, and had fun just for the heck of it. And with the fun I enjoyed the sound of each word, each sentence, each perfect tricolon. This is all I have to say: "It's Roman, look!"

My real love stories—by now I am convinced that this is what I am writing—are about living languages. My friend Shane would perhaps remind me that if by "living" I mean a language that we speak and write today, Latin is perfectly alive: He corresponds in Latin with different people. But that is his opinion.

We have become polyglots in Spain, it seems. It is the EEC's fault. But people there still ask me why I learned Polish (nobody cares about it in the United States, obviously). I never know what to say. People would like me to respond that my grandmother was from Poland, or something short, concise, and tangible. Well, she wasn't. This is the least tangible of my stories.

My aunt took me to Poland when I was 13. It was one of the first authorized trips to a Communist country during Franco's life. My aunt had to go to Poland because of a religious promise. This is a story for another time, and it sounds bizarre because it is bizarre. So she took me, but she communicated in French and once in Latin with a priest. I did not communicate at all. It was a fun trip. The country was so mysterious, so frugal, so romantic. I thought my life had changed forever after I went to a concert at Zelazowa Wola, Chopin's birthplace. Everybody was taken there, almost by government orders, but that mattered little because I wanted to go. I thought again that my life had changed forever after I saw Leonardo's "Lady with Ermine" at the Czartoryski Museum in Krakow. Everybody seemed to be so educated, so polite; everybody kissed your hand and called you "madam." And oh, that language that I could not understand, that insinuating, seductive, sibilant language!

In my first year at the university in Madrid—I was 17—I saw that Polish was taught and I decided to learn it. I think my memories of Poland had little to do with my decision. But it was there, and it seemed a pity not to take it. For no better reason. I have always been proud of my tendency toward profitless activities. Learning Polish turned out to be totally profitless, but extremely beneficial. *Doña* Gabriela Makowiecka taught me Polish for five years, and I was her only student for the last four. I doubt they paid her to teach just one student, but she stuck to it, and so did I. I admired her. I was totally shy in front of her, because her encyclopedic knowledge overwhelmed me. Her classes were serious and very traditional, homework and exams (for me, alone!) included. I learned my grammar and I had a first taste of Sienkiewicz, Mickiewicz, and even Lesmian and Tuwim. For years I struggled with the numerals twelve and twenty, *dwanaście* and *dwadzieścia* in Polish, and every time *pani* (Mrs.) Makowiecka made gentle but stern fun of my "incomprehensible" mix-ups.

Pani Makowiecka was a true Old World lady. She was very skinny and dressed with impeccable sobriety. She truly knew inside-out several languages. She taught classes every year at the Sorbonne and in Krakow, as well as in Madrid. She had written an excellent study of Luzán's *Poetics*, a thick 18th-century treaty dreaded by students of Spanish literature as "*un plomo*," a piece of lead, but quite interesting for scholars, who valued highly *pani* Makowiecka's book. The academic community loved her, and the diplomatic community respected her. I never found out why she settled in

Spain; she never said and I never asked. She lived in a very plush building in Velázquez, one of the most chic neighborhoods in Madrid. Her house was packed with books in triple file, floor to ceiling, including hallways. In her apartment there were also *pan* (Mr.) Makowiecki, her husband, and Paca, the maid. *Pani* Makowiecka was an elegant cook (I remember a trout aspic and the tiniest strawberries), but Paca seemed indispensable and omnipresent. Next to *pani* Makowiecka's serenity, her husband was like a hive of bees on a summer afternoon. He was witty, but annoying; kind, but irascible; extremely brilliant, but very talkative. He had the terrifying habit of switching languages in mid-speech; from Spanish to Polish, from Polish to French, and back to Spanish. Sometimes he used a Latin dictum for color, and rare was the time I did not feel deep humiliation because I got so, so lost in the conversation, and he knew it.

I identified the language with my teacher. I could see *doña* Gabriela's precision in the prefixes of the verbs; her versatility in the lyricism of the nouns; her poise in the national epics; her tenderness in the incredibly disarming diminutives; her charm in the sensuousness of the sounds. I really fell in love with the language, and I idolized *doña* Gabriela. The Polish language and she are one in my mind and in my heart. Sometimes now I read Polish out loud because its whispers lullaby and soothe me; I think of *doña* Gabriela, and the memory of her tender dignity helps me to regain my composure.

My first recollection of anything French is two books with worn-out blue covers, *Cours de Langue et Civilisation Françaises*, published by the *Librarie Hachette* in Paris. I have always liked the sound of "*Librarie Hachette, Paris.*" I look at the books sometimes now. They have clear grammatical explanations, little vignettes representing famous places—*le Panthéon, les Invalides, la Tour Eiffel*; they have photos with their captions—*que de cafés à Paris!, le bassin du Luxembourg, la grotte miraculeuse de Lourdes* (so many cafes in Paris!, the Luxembourg Basin, the miraculous cave of Lourdes); they have songs—*Sur le Pont d'Avignon, Gentille Alouette, Carillon de Vendôme* (On the Avignon Bridge, Gentle Lark, the Carillon of Vendôme); they have my father's glosses in his elegant, exquisite handwriting—*un couche-tard, trasnochador* (a night owl); *friandise, golosina* (a tidbit). I did not use these books to study French. My aunt sent us, my brothers and me, to take French lessons with Juani Benedicto, who must have taught French to everyone in town. Juani taught in her apartment in a room with cracking wood floors and hard chairs, and narrow benches along the corridor walls that served as a waiting room between classes. She was a tiny woman, and even then I realized how peculiar it was that she made her mouth round every time she spoke, as if she spoke Spanish with a French shape. I did not learn a lot then. I was not interested in anything French, because my aunt adored France, and I could not like what she liked.

When I was 18 I met Claudia, an American, in Germany. My English was bad, I was shy, and she was kind. We spoke in French. My French was as bad as my English, but it was a lingua franca for both and I did not feel so embarrassed at my mistakes. We spoke and we wrote in French. "*Un ami, c'est quelqu'un qui t'aime*" (a friend is someone who loves you), she wrote to me once. Had I known then what love was, I would have known that I was in love. But that came later. Claudia came to visit me in Spain. After she left, we corresponded frequently. I spent hours composing long letters to her in English and sometimes still in French, surrounded by dictionaries worthless to help me express an intensity of feeling that I could not really understand. Suddenly Claudia stopped writing and she disappeared. It was then that my urge to learn became pure passion. I read Proust with frenzy, and memorized Yourcenar, Shakespeare, and Whitman; I summoned up the remembrance of things past and sighed the lack of many a thing I sought.

I got a master's in English, another in Classics, and by the time I accepted a job offer in Italy, my Italian came exclusively from Monteverdi, from Verdi and Puccini, and, of course, from Mozart. I am sure that fate took me to Pesaro, Rossini's birthplace, and fate brought Claudia back to me when I was leaving for Italy. I should have known, using opera as a textbook as I was doing, that nothing good could come out of so many *addios* (goodbyes). But when Claudia arrived that summer, I could not remember a single opera ending. I could not remember Tosca jumping off Castel Sant'Angelo, or Violetta's consumption, or Butterfly's suicide. I could only remember my arias full of passion and desire, my exhilarating cavatine, my love duets—both parts. I was in love and this time I knew it, and it seemed completely according to the laws of art to start my life in love in Italian.

I learned Italian to bargain grades with my students and their families; to quibble with the banks, the police, the landlady, and the post office; to ask for coins instead of candy or toothpicks in lieu of change at the supermarket; I learned Italian to rent an apartment, to buy train tickets, and to dispute wrongly added bills. I learned Italian to laugh with my friend Teresa in her kitchen and to take part in serious disputes about pesto with or without garlic, and the superior flavor of pecorino sardo over pecorino romano. I learned Italian because I had decided we had to be there, so that I could see all the Roman ruins in the world and my lover could see all the art in the world. But my comfort with the language and my acceptance of the peculiar cultural habits that came with it were not enough; we were pinched, harassed, insulted, pushed, mistreated, and abused. Claudia was unhappy. I should have remembered then my opera endings, but that did not happen until many years later.

I learned my languages for love, but I loved in English, and that, I suppose, makes all the difference in the world. I studied many, many years of English in Spain. I went against my aunt's wishes and took it in high school. At the end she won, because I followed her advice and got a degree in English Philology at the university. I cannot say that I enjoyed my studies. Reading medieval sermons had no relationship with reading Claudia's letters, and writing papers about *The Narrative of Arthur Gordon Pym* had nothing to do with staying up at night to write her long missives, struggling with every idea and every preposition. My aunt said—this was years ago, before Spain joined the EEC—that English had a lot of potential, that it offered "many exits," as she put it. I guess she was right after all.

My years in Italy with Claudia made me believe that I knew English. We played, we laughed, we learned about each other in English. I could express tenderness in English more easily, perhaps, than I could do it in my own language. I did not care about grammatical correctness anymore, because I thought that I could finally communicate, despite my troubles with prepositions. But the first time I had to speak with her brother, in Queens, I wanted to cry; and when we went to visit her friend Bonnie, who is from Tennessee, I thought I was going to lose my mind. Until we moved to New York, I had tried to speak good English with a good accent. I meant that seriously. My first year in New York was, however, a linguistic nightmare. I had never felt so much anguish with a foreign language. And I wanted to master it so desperately. After a while, what I had considered total grammatical anarchy ceased to bother me. I overcame my initial puzzle at so many accents, and decided to keep my own. I knew I was doing well when people began to mistake Claudia for me and me for her over the phone. She has never had a recognizable "American" accent: That is why she blends so beautifully in any foreign language. I have an accent (Americans who know Spanish talk to me in my language, without bothering to inquire) and I am keeping it, in part because my accent reminds me of the contradiction I live every day and I am amused by it.

"Stout as a horse, affectionate, haughty, electrical" (Whitman, 1975, p. 171). My friend Shane says that it is in Whitman ("Song of Myself") where he sees the essence of American English, so non-Latin, so wide, so un-European. I have read Whitman a lot during the past two years in Virginia. I delight in English: It soothes me, it comforts my soul, it reassures my body. Pecans in Georgia and Granny's pound cake; orange trees in Florida; Central Park and summer concerts; the Triboro bridge on foot; Astoria for olive oil and Atlantic Avenue for spices; our beautiful apartment in Manhattan and our projects for a long life together; there is love and tenderness in my landscapes, and I always think of them in English. Claudia speaks now with a different accent; she is still the reason for keeping mine. I think of my friend Susan, and thank her for her insight.

In the small town in Virginia where I live, people ask me constantly about my accent. I have been trying hard to emend my pronunciation. But I have been unsuccessful. It's been in these past two years (my own long "sessions of sweet silent thought") that I have realized how great a part of me is my own language. I claim Spanish as mine, now more than ever. I have not been in my country during these two years. I have lived in exile from everything that was dear to me, in the middle of beautiful scenery, alone and isolated. Communicating with the birds and the trees has been easier than communicating with the people in town: They do not like my accent. I have memorized poems, again, in Spanish, opening my lips to pronounce the lines silently, as the medieval monks recited their prayers. Cernuda (1983, p. 172) has given words to my despair: "... *donde penas y dichas no sean más que nombres, cielo y tierra nativos en torno de un recuerdo*" ("Where sorrow and happiness are nothing but native names, sky, and land around a memory"); Garcia Lorca (1955, p. 100) has given words to my acceptance of the inevitable: "*¿Qué voy a hacer? ¿ordenar los paisajes? ¿ordenar los amores que luego son fotografías ... ?*" ("What am I to do? Tidy up landscapes? Tidy up loves that later become photographs ... ?"); Borges (1985, p. 173) has given words to my strength: "*Sé que en la eternidad perdura y arde lo mucho y lo precioso que he perdido*" ("I know that all the many precious things I have lost, burn and endure in eternity"); Machado (1975, p. 151) has returned to me the flavors of my childhood: "*Una larga carretera entre grises peñascales ... zarzas, malezas, jarales*" ("a long road among grey rocky hills ... brambles, brushwood, scrub").

I have remembered here the pride I felt when I was growing up for "*la palabra bien dicha*," (the word well said). I have remembered my grandfather Tino, weaving fabulous stories in the kitchen with his deep voice and his exquisite Castilian. I have remembered my grandfather Pedro who, in our long walks in the countryside, taught me how to love plants, their uses and their names—*ajedrea* (savory) for colds and olives, *espliego* (lavender) for ointments and its scent, *aliaga* (gorse) just for its beauty. I have remembered my father's voice teaching me how to swim. I have remembered my mother, who created her own terms of endearment for me and my brothers (I was her "*píldoreta*," her little pill).

Claudia still calls me "*nena*" (baby) and her, I do not have to remember. She writes to me rare but precious letters in her wonderful, lovely Spanish. She tells me about her garden and the new joints she has learned in her classes. She uses words that I have not heard before: exotic English flowers and unfamiliar carpentry terms. And she asks for recipes: the cheese spread with sherry that we made in Italy, and my aunt's soup with squash and cheese. I cry and smile, and laugh and scream, and love and hate, when I read—I can hear her voice so clearly. Her Spanish breaks the silence of my days, gives flesh and meaning to the poems I read daily, and softens my loneliness. I still write to her in English, with the same accent.

References

Borges, J. L. (1985). *"Ewigkeit." Obra poetica 1923–1977.* Madrid: Alianza Tres/ Emece.
Cernuda, L. (1983). *"Donde habite el olvido." La realidad y el deseo.* Madrid: F.C.E.
Garcia Lorca, F. (1955). *"Vuelta a la ciudad." Poeta en Nueva York.* New York: Grove Press.
Machado, A. (1975). *"Amanecer de otono." Campos de Castilla.* Madrid: Espasa Calpe.
Whitman, W. (1975). *Song of myself.* Middlesex: Penguin Books.

Part V

CLOSE ENCOUNTERS WITH OTHER CULTURES: LEARNING LANGUAGE WHILE LIVING ABROAD

More than other parts, "Close Encounters" hones in on linguistic realities and specific properties of languages, such as differences in pronunciation, tones, body language, and how meanings get changed in translation. Readers can feel the cultural clashes and the bonds as writers describe their experiences living with people in different cultures.

Doug Millison's (Watson's father) essay is well suited in its complexity of feeling to follow the above meditations on languages and love. Millison's journey into Chinese begins by helping his future Chinese wife learn English. His piece explores the impact this has had on the image he holds of himself as a white American male, husband, and father in a cross-cultural, interracial marriage. The deeper he gets into learning a foreign language, the more he discovers depths in himself, and in his native culture, of which he was previously unaware.

Mancuso explores the concept of "speaking the culture" in her piece about feeling silenced while on vacation in Mexico with her Mexican fiancé (now husband), Rodgers, whose interpretations of the event are represented in italics. Language acquisition meets feminism and psychology when Mancuso, in her fierce desire to be heard, unconsciously shifts her "woman warrior" stance to one the men, with whom she was dealing in the particular context, could relate to better: the traditional female role of wife and mother. The result, as the next author, Linda Petrucelli, also discovers, is the need to change oneself through the difficult attempt of learning another language. Petrucelli compares learning Taiwanese in Taiwan to a process of self and spiritual exploration. Her piece also provides interesting insights into language ideology in Taiwan, which is revealing of how inextricably tied linguistic policies are to personal and national identity.

My experiences learning Japanese as an adult without formal language instruction provide a different perspective on the assertion made by George Jochnowitz, that "Adults have to be taught grammar." Although I "learned" a foreign language (grammar) in schools for years, I could not speak it. It wasn't until I lived in Japan as an adult, where I received no formal language instruction, that I was able to use Japanese in a meaningful way. (I agree with Susan Stocker that wanting to speak is a strong motivator.) My piece, which closes the volume, focuses on the relationship between language and gender identity. On a very deep, partly even preverbal, layer my experiences being foreign in language and society mingle with my perceptions of being a woman as I observed and experienced it in English. I describe my process of acquiring implicit understandings of my place both as a foreigner in Japan and as a woman in my own culture. Perceptions of self as a white American woman shifted, along with how I spoke in different sociolinguistic contexts.

22

Learning Chinese

DOUG MILLISON

A mutual friend introduced me to Alice. Born in Shanghai, raised in Beijing, she arrived in Berkeley about a year before we met in 1981. "I know you'll like these two *jolies Pekinoises* in my husband's English conversation class," my French friend Isabelle told me. She arranged a party so I could meet them.

Xiao Hong, tall and earnest, looked like she might have stepped out of a Socialist Realist propaganda poster. She walked away toward the buffet as soon as possible after Isabelle introduced me.

Alice stayed, but she didn't seem to have much to say, not to me at least. What little she did say barely broke the surface of her halting, heavily accented English. Hair curled in soft, dark waves framed a pretty, heart-shaped face and kind eyes. I wanted to get to know her better. Isabelle helped me bump into her over the next few weeks that summer at lunch and parties.

Alice lived and worked as a housekeeper and companion for Vera, a 104-year-old White Russian immigrant gynecologist, ancient but still kicking. They lived in Vera's 1920s bungalow on Berkeley's north side. Since she remained reluctant to go out with me, I offered to help Alice with her English. I went to Vera's house one evening a week. We'd work on her English and her schoolwork, chat for a while, then I'd drive back to my studio across town. By Thanksgiving, I visited twice a week. By Christmas she was feeding me dinner each time.

Language-learning meta-talk dominated our conversation at first: definitions, explanations, illustrations, context. I explained, Alice repeated words and phrases, practiced pronunciation, composed sentences. As her English improved, I started learning more about her.

President Nixon's mid-1970s China diplomacy led to Alice's presence in Berkeley. Her father's older sister fled China in 1947 and settled in Berkeley. Auntie sponsored Alice's student visa application as soon as the two countries made that possible.

I talked about my life and hopes, too. With each new bit of information, each step deeper into self-disclosure, we were falling in love. Despite my foreign language background, I felt no real desire to learn Chinese from her. My job was to help her learn English. I would introduce her, through the language, to America, her new home. I saw helping her acquire English as a way of opening myself up, too. I was giving her the key she could use to unlock me. Keeping English as our language also gave me the upper hand, let me control her access to my world, although I didn't think of it in those terms.

I knew what it took to learn a foreign language. I studied French in nursery school, a little in elementary school, in high school, and graduated with a B.A. in French from the University of California at Berkeley. I studied Spanish for several years in high school and college. I crammed a year of Japanese into a 10-week intensive summer language program at Berkeley. As a GI, I had learned some bits and pieces of Korean. I was a good English teacher, too. I knew how to approach an English word or phrase from one angle, then from another. I showed Alice how to study definitions and relate a word to synonyms, antonyms, and idioms. I knew the pitfalls of homonyms and mispronunciations: "Doug-bow-wow? Or Doug-quack-quack?" was the standing joke about my name among our Chinese friends ("Doug" sounds like "dog" and "duck"). I provided the background for words and phrases in a newspaper or magazine, on radio or television. I spoke slowly and enunciated clearly. I delighted in the flicker in her eyes that preceded an "I've-got-it!" flash.

It worked. By the end of the following summer, when she transferred to San Jose State University for nursing school, she was ready for me to follow her. Halfway through fall session, I asked her to marry me. We married at the beginning of the new year.

We faced the usual struggle to get to know each other and to live together. Between us opened the language gap. Friction and misunderstandings led to the arguments and tears common to all newlyweds, but ours felt even more difficult to fathom and amend.

A year and a half after our marriage, we traveled to China on a delayed honeymoon, a chance for me to meet her parents. I began to see and understand something of how things worked in her family, in the Chinese culture and social system.

I saw the tenderness and intimacy between Alice and her parents after a three-year absence. This bond had kept them close years before, when Alice roamed the Chinese countryside during her brief tenure as a *hong bing* Red Guard before they kicked her out for a bad class background. It held her family together when the Party forced Alice and her elder sister out of Beijing to the countryside with other urban youths in the early 1970s, when Chairman Mao saw the Cultural Revolution spinning out of control. I thought of the contrast with my own nuclear family turned nuclear bomb, where the pieces kept flying apart after the explosion of my parents' divorce.

I had lived overseas before. I spent a year in the Republic of Korea, courtesy of the U.S. Army, in the early 1970s. Later, I studied for a year in France, working on my undergraduate degree.

In France I savored the subtle differences in food, sounds, smells, architecture, people. The abyss between what I found in South Korea and my previous experience shook me. But I could always withdraw into my American GI cocoon, inside one of those American culture bubbles that dotted the Korean landscape and comforted us with stateside Army life—the PX, the Enlisted Man's Club, the movies, the food, Armed Forces Radio, the *Pacific Stars & Stripes* newspaper.

In China with Alice, I was immersed. We lived mostly with relatives—at her parents' apartment in Beijing, at her grandmother's old house on Shanghai's Nanjing Dong Lu, with her aunt and uncle in Hangzhou. We lodged at Chinese hotels that were not cookie-cutter Holiday Inn environments.

The Chinese language presented a formidable barrier—no alphabet to give the semblance of familiarity, no aural hooks on the radio or television. Alice couldn't translate fast enough or to the degree I wanted. I wanted to know what that billboard was selling right now, what those people were talking about, in detail, at the next table. What was the anchorman reporting on the evening news, what did that song's lyrics say? I sat on the periphery of Alice's conversations with her family. I had never sought this level of cultural engagement in Korea, where I learned only enough of the Korean–English pidgin to navigate the R & R demimonde. I had taken it for granted in France. Now I felt like a tourist in China. Didn't I deserve an insider's view?

I returned to the United States determined to learn Chinese, but my career realities and Alice's school challenges intervened. By the time Alice graduated with her nursing degree the following year, an opportunity emerged to take us back to China. She found a job with Project Hope, an international medical foundation that was helping to establish China's first four-year baccalaureate degree nursing school since liberation in 1949.

We went to Xian, China's capital during the Tang dynasty golden age, when it was called Chang'an—about 1,200 kilometers southwest of Beijing.

Alice contracted to spend nine months as a liaison for Project Hope nurse educators at Xian *Yi Ke Da Xue*, Xian Medical University (XMU). She would help develop curricula for the new nursing degree program and train the Chinese nurses to be the school's teachers and administrators. As soon as we settled into the Zhaodaisuo Hostel, I started exploring the campus and surrounding neighborhood. As I told myself, "I'm no tourist, I live in this town," I realized I had to learn Chinese. I thought back to a time some years before, near the end of my school year in France, when I enjoyed a moment of linguistic glory one afternoon in a small, dimly lit working class bistro near the *Gare du Nord* in Paris. I nursed a glass of red wine and eavesdropped on a group of Frenchmen at the other end of the bar. One of them nodded his head toward me. An expression of disgust twisted his face. "Who's the tourist and what's he doing in our place?" I piped up, in my best titi Parisian accent, "*Suis pas touriste, j'habite Paname.*" Suddenly I found myself within the golden circle of their company. The accent, the casual use of the slang *Paname* instead of *Paris*, the faux-Gallic shrug and nod of the head—they bought me drinks the rest of the afternoon and refused to let me stand a round.

I wanted that same feeling of acceptance in China. I wanted to join those who could scornfully exclude foreign tourists, especially the Americans I saw running rampant with their fistfuls of traveler's checks and their demands for service. I wanted to be appreciated for the effort I made to learn their language. I wanted to astonish the Chinese with my fluency and delight them with my wit. I wanted to be part of the family.

I was jealous of the American English teachers we met at XMU when we joined them at the off-campus restaurant. They knew the Chinese names of everything worth eating and joked with the waitress. I learned some phrases. "*Wo de mingzi shi Dao ge la si.*" (My name is Douglas.) "*Wo shi meiguo ren.*" (I am American.) "*Wo airen shi zhongguo ren.*" (My wife is Chinese.) I could introduce myself. I taught myself to count money. Now I could haggle in the market.

I learned more words and phrases. At the open market near XMU I ordered *rou bing*-flat, round bread, griddle-fried and wrapped around a chunk of roast pork—the way I liked it. "*Bu yao fei rou,*" I commanded. "No fat meat." Self-preservation motivated me. Without these instructions, the merchant would honor me with the prize portion: the juiciest slice of the fattest part for the foreign guest.

I couldn't delve deep enough. I still felt like an outsider.

The medical school dean's brother-in-law was a big shot at *Yu Yan Xue Yuan*, the Beijing Language Institute. Dean Fang offered to arrange for me to enter a Chinese college preparatory language immersion course. Instead of going through normal channels, we did it the Chinese way: We used *guanxi* connections to go through the back door. I moved to Beijing to study. Alice stayed in Xian for the remaining months of her Project Hope contract.

I lived with my mother- and father-in-law, Alice's older sister, her husband, and their two-year-old son in a three-bedroom apartment on the *Hang Kong Xue Yuan* (Beijing University of Aeronautics and Astronautics) campus 10 minutes by bicycle from *Yu Yan Xue Yuan.* I had my own tiny room, with a twin bed, a desk, a chest of drawers, and just enough room to walk from the doorway down to the desk and execute a tight pirouette if the spirit took me.

Freed from a job and housework, I focused on school. I spent four hours in class each morning and at least four hours on homework each evening. The remaining waking hours I devoted to family meals, roaming the city by bicycle to practice my Chinese, and television. Within a few weeks, I spoke Chinese better than my sister-in-law Yin Hua and her husband Wei Ke spoke English; following the "dominant language capability in any two-language relationship wins" rule, I used Chinese to communicate with them from that point forward. Alice's parents still spoke English better than I spoke Chinese—it took me several months to catch up.

The program I entered at *Yu Yan Xue Yuan* took foreign students with no prior knowledge of Chinese and taught them enough in two years to let them go on to complete degree programs at Chinese universities. Some would stay at *Yu Yan Xue Yuan* and pursue advanced studies in Chinese language and literature. Most would move on to other schools to study other subjects.

I completed the first year of a two-year program. I learned to read and write the nearly 2,000 *hanzi* characters necessary to tackle contemporary magazines, newspapers, and books, plus basic grammar, pronunciation, and conversation. With the aid of a Chinese dictionary I could pick my way, slowly, through the *People's Daily.* Television started making sense, although each TV program presented a new world of vocabulary. I did best with programs from the U.S. and Europe dubbed in Chinese. *Little House on the Prairie* and the BBC's *Sherlock Holmes* were my favorites. I talked a lot, in a rather stilted, textbook idiom. I was acquiring critical mass to blossom into a more natural, conversational fluency.

I felt myself changing.

My face, mouth, lips, and throat muscles stretched then strengthened after initial, feeble resistance to taking new shapes to form new sounds. My ears tuned to a new pitch of discrimination to untangle the four-tone *shengyin* system that made the evening television news a melody in the mouth of the newscaster no matter what burden of crisis, crime, or propaganda the words had to carry, or rendered a soccer match play-by-play into musical comedy. *Shengyin* layered onto spoken Chinese yet another network of signs to decipher. *Shengyin* let *"ma"* mean, depending on which of the four tones it took, and which character I used to write it:

ma (even tone) = "mother"
ma (rising tone) = "hemp"
ma (dipping tone) = "horse"
ma (falling tone) = "curse you"

I disciplined myself to endure hours at my desk as I memorized and copied *hanzi* late into winter evenings after the building's steam heat turned off. I sat swaddled in cotton long underwear, goosedown pants, jeans, flannel shirt, goosedown jacket liner, and parka.

Each new *hanzi* opened another door. I traced inscriptions along corridors that carried me ever closer to the heart of this marvelous, many-chambered edifice of the new Chinese me.

I was the dutiful son-in-law, learning Chinese to better communicate with and understand my wife and my wife's family, their country, and culture.

I learned the *bu shou* root characters that combined and recombined, sometimes in altered forms, to make up the individual *hanzi* ideograms. *Bu shou* did not constitute an alphabet, but these reusable components did represent a key to core meanings to guide me through the thicket of brush-strokes and characters.

I forgot myself entirely as I watched the meanings of an individual *hanzi* shift as it combined with other characters to form two-character words and four-character idioms, in the shuttling from page to page in my Chinese-only and Chinese-English/English-Chinese dictionaries. Family, future, fortune retreated beyond my circle of lamp light as I copied *hanzi* in precise stroke order, filling page after page of quadrille-ruled onionskin.

I saw before me the endlessly pleasing prospect of exploring a horizonless landscape of meaning, character by character, word by word, phrase by phrase, paragraph by paragraph, text by text. Beyond contemporary Chinese lay the misty vistas of classical Chinese, yet another foreign language unto itself with its own syntax and specialized vocabulary—as distant from modern Chinese as Chaucer lies from Thomas Pynchon—written in the old characters that had been simplified (in terms of brush-strokes) in the modern Chinese I studied. I dreamed undiscovered continents of literature, history, philosophy. I wanted to lose myself in those dreamy landscapes.

Ever since I learned my first few French words from Mrs. Drum at nursery school, I sensed the presence of a truer me that I could find and express as I loosened the bonds of my familiar existence and moved from my mother tongue into a foreign language.

With my guitar I had sometimes been able to voice this longing, but I wanted to do it with words. In the otherworldly accents of Spanish, Japanese, French, and now Chinese, I thought I heard echoes of a Platonic me, the self that cast shadows on the cave wall of my mundane existence. I seemed to discover a more authentic self as I used other languages to examine, twist, test, transform what I had learned growing up in the dreary swamplands of Louisiana, in the yellow dust West Texas caliche, in the Arizona desert where *saguaro* cactuses open their hands in prickly greeting and point always to the sky.

Family momentum pushed us east to California, away from China. The time came for me to go back to the United States and take up my responsibilities as a husband and new father. Alice had returned to California to give birth to our son a couple of months before I finished my year at *Yu Yan Xue Yuan.*

Back in the United States, I found work again as a journalist. I would use my Chinese to talk with Alice and her family as they emigrated and joined us in California over the next few years. I would be able to reinforce their efforts to help our son learn Chinese.

Learning Chinese enabled a new regime of intimacy with Alice and her family. It also brings what I perceive as an expectation to act according to her family's unspoken rules of engagement. No longer am I an untutored barbarian and thus exempt.

When I first traveled with Alice in China, I experienced the strange feeling of being a foreigner, *wai guo ren* (person from outside the country). I hadn't felt that in France, where everybody looked more or less like me. In Korea, we American GIs remained oblivious to what the Koreans thought of us. In China, children in the street giggled and called me *lao wai* (a familiar form of *wai guo ren*). Less flattering were those who pointed and said *da bizi* (big nose). A few whispered *yang gueizi* (foreign devil). Learning Chinese gave me the power to stop this simply by opening my mouth, engaging in a conversation, taking myself out of the foreigner box, opening the way to relationship. And it brought me fully under the roof of Alice's *jia,* the family. I became a *jia li ren* (a "person inside the family") in a way I hadn't been before.

Now I know why Alice defers to her elder sister's wishes, contradictory and confusing though they might sometimes be, and why I must defer to her wishes, too. I understand why Alice avoids saying "no" directly to her parents, to her sister, and to her father's elder sister, who lives a few blocks from us. I know that I am not supposed to say no to them directly, either. After all, Auntie's approval had calmed the worries that gripped Alice's parents when they first heard she was dating a *wai guo ren*.

Like a good Chinese husband, I have learned to evade a question rather than put myself in a situation where I might have to answer in the negative, to change the subject or proactively offer what I want to do or can do instead of waiting for an unwelcome request. When all else fails, I know I must give in gracefully, a lesson I'm still perfecting. Evasion, submission, and yielding still grate against my sense of myself as an outspoken American who says what he means in a culture that values emotional transparence and openness. Learning Chinese and getting a glimpse of America through Alice's lens has helped me begin to see the limitations of this personal myth.

Alice and her family expend impressive emotional energies to keep from expressing strong feelings in their faces or tone of voice. They avoid actions or words calculated to shock or offend—no words today that might wound or might have to be taken back and eaten tomorrow. They know how to *chi ku* (eat bitterness) and *baoquan mianzi* (save face).

I often find myself asking Alice to help me understand what she's feeling, what she wants me to do, because, as I say, "I can't read your mind." To her, I am as easy to read as a child. I am aware that the set of my jaw or the line of my lips can and will trigger speculation about the possible sources of my displeasure. Again and again I find myself apologizing for words spoken in anger or in haste, without consideration and revision to avoid offense in its manifold manifestations.

I've learned the language. I've only begun to understand and implement these rules of engagement. I continue the quest, negotiating the shifting zones of self circumscribed by words and the past, to find and express a self free to explore, create, love, connect, from one moment to the next— the authentic me.

23

Speaking the Culture

CAROLINA MANCUSO AND
DAVID RODGERS

David: You have reached 718–555–7726.
Carolina: ¡Hola! Gracias por llamar. Favor de dejar su mensaje
    después del tono.
David: ¡Órale pues!
Carolina: ¡Adiós!

Callers who get our New York City home answering machine sometimes hang up and call again. They're puzzled by the trilingual message: two standard dialects—English and Spanish—and one nonstandard dialect—Chicano. The ones who know me often exclaim that they had no idea I speak Spanish so "fluently." David especially likes that one. A Chilango, that is, a native of Mexico City, he's watched me struggle all the years we've been together to get my Spanish up and running. And for this message, where we switched who speaks which language from our earlier ones, he not only delivers the English and the Chicano, but has also written the script I carefully read into the tape! I fear it apes a language practice tape—de-lib-er-ate, e-nun-ci-ated—but everyone (maybe kindly) says no. Well, if it works, it's the accent that does the trick.

I grew up in a bilingual household, my mother an immigrant from Italy, my father born here only because he was the youngest of many siblings. My place in the family—the last of five, and seven years behind the others—insured that I would not grow up bilingual. My mother abandoned the effort after watching her older children's carefully taught Italian wiped away by American public schools. She swore (as at many things American, including the spelling rules of English) not to waste her time again.

I was born in México, D.F., the ancient Tenochtitlán—known to outsiders as Mexico City. I grew up bilingual in a dual-language household, my mother an immigrant from the United States, my father born in Guanajuato, Guanajuato, México, as was my brother. As the youngest, I got to be born and raised in México, D.F.—sadly destined to become the world's largest metropolis. Yet in my time, it insured that I would grow up bilingual and bicultural. My father swore at many things American; however, he did so following the norms of Standard English.

Though I didn't learn Italian, I must have inherited the propensity, for I achieved high proficiency during four years of high school Latin, three of French, and two of college Russian. Throughout, my friends and I made great sport of convincing new guys that we were French. I picked up accents easily, too, confusing people with the true origins of my Southern Italian crossroads ethnicity. No doubt that facility grew through theater work in high school, college, and later professionally. But all this language development was also supported through the modeling of my similarly capable siblings, who, during my childhood, sought their own multilingual accomplishments, bringing home Russian and Arabic, among others.

Gradually, however, like so many others with school-based language learning, I stopped speaking them all: the intensity of working and raising a child alone, the limits of exposure, the slippage of memory, and then discouragement at losing the "knack." When a friend convinced me to take an evening class in Italian, I rejoiced at proof of how much I had managed to glean as a child. I retained, however, about 2%, one of which was packed into a song.

Then I met David, who stirred my desire to reclaim my facility with languages. His bicultural home life had made him perfectly bilingual from his very first sentence: "*Quiero* crackers." Suddenly I had a focused purpose for doing what I'd wanted to do since moving to New York many years before. And Spanish was so close to Italian, after all.

I began studying in various settings and, it felt, losing everything soon after each workshop or class came to an end. By the time I reenrolled somewhere, I was starting nearly from scratch. I can easily lay claim to the world's record for Most Repetitions of Beginning Spanish and have not, to this day, completed the Intermediate. For the eight-year midlife stint in graduate school, I added another excuse to the list: My brain, like Gary Larson's cartoon student, was simply "full." And now an even bigger one looms: My brain is simply aging.

While it is widely recognized that adults lose much of the facility for language acquisition that is characteristic of young children, I wonder how much is contributed by living in a culture where multiple languages are not valued and even suppressed. How much do monolingual attitudes push the atrophy? Surely, if your brain has expanded to two languages in childhood and adolescence, learning others must not present the obstacles the rest of us face.

Not only my experience, but also what I've observed in teaching Native Language Spanish and ESL at Newcomers High School in Queens, a school for immigrants from 45 different countries, has convinced me that total immersion may be the only truly effective way to acquire and internalize a third, fourth, or fifth language.

Despite David's willing assistance and my believable accents and once near-fluencies, I've lost confidence from repeated learning and un-learning. I have felt silenced by dwindling skills, fear of error and embarrassment, and confusion at the loss of an ability I so loved. Each failure builds upon the last, at times sending me right back to early childhood, to that kitchen table with my mother and my aunts passing homemade cookies and sisterly secrets over my head. I hear the lyrical native Italian as song, catch a few words, grasp intent in a gestalt of language. There was pleasure then in both knowing and not-knowing, and that early language phase appears to continue to yield hidden fruit even, as explained below, in the most trying circumstances.

It was not my first visit to México, but the first since David and I had begun a committed relationship. Gradually, I had been noticing my deep connection to Mexican culture through my Italian roots. Despite differences, there were startling similarities, among them warmth and hospitality and the emphasis on family and friends. In this, my second visit, I was determined to take advantage of total immersion. My feminist soul bristled at the thought of subsuming my independence, at least on a public level. With gritted teeth, I faced my self-condemnation that no, I had not learned a speck more Spanish since my last trip, and was linguistically dependent upon—much as I loved him—a man.

After a few days in México, D.F., the three of us—David, my teenage son, Sean, and I—planned to set out for Guanajuato, David's father's native city and residence. We were to stay with close family friends, and I was madly brushing up my limited skills and buoying my fractured linguistic courage. In the car rental office, we encountered mismanagement and a six-hour inconvenience, and my teeth ground again at being unable to join in the heated discussion between the manager and David. A single parent in charge of all public battles for so long, my identity was stung. But I shrugged it off, eager to move on and unsuspecting of the intense encounter with the deep ramifications of language, culture, and gender just ahead.

It was not my first visit to the United States but the first since I was old enough to appreciate the cultural distinctions—even if at a subconscious level. I became aware of my deep connection to New York City culture through my mother's roots. What I saw in New York was close to México, D.F. in terms of large cities, and as such, even at age 11, I had no difficulty in handling the city culture. We stayed at the Picadilly Hotel on 45th Street, half a block from the main action of Times Square. What perplexed me was that I could not equate the American culture I had encountered in the border city of El Paso with what I was presently facing in New York.

After a few days in the city, the four of us—my parents, my older brother, and I—took the New Jersey Transit train from the Hoboken station to Denville, where my mother had grown up. We were on our way to spend Thanksgiving with my great-aunt. It was my first Thanksgiving in the United States as well as with extended family. Auntie Ban had invited her two brothers and their families to join in the feast. I eagerly took in all the conversations and stories, which, of course, revealed more of my familial identity. That experience deepened my understanding of American culture and reinforced my bicultural upbringing.

When we hit the chunk of metal, it was the one time I wasn't sitting in the front seat watching. Eased by the well-kept, lightly trafficked six-lane highway, I had slipped into a pleasant semi-stupor brought on by a lunch of *mole enchiladas* and memories of childhood backseat rides sparked by the Spanish Burma Shave signs along the way. The lifts and dips of the hill country had prevented David from seeing the object earlier. In the precious instant when we might have swerved, tractor-trailers bordered us in each lane. I literally didn't know what hit us.

At roadside, we saw that the car was dripping, nearly streaming, gas, so we jumped out and put a safe distance between us and the growing puddle. David rushed out to retrieve the metal culprit before the incident could be repeated. He returned with a monstrous hunk roughly a foot and a half in all dimensions with a sharp fin slick enough to slice a gas tank, probably from the wreckage of another hapless vehicle. It had flipped in the air after we hit it and could have devastated a car behind us. Worse, it began to appear a deliberate weapon: David had seen a *niño* running into the field. Adrenaline focused our silent stares at the sinister thing, nestled in the tall grass, twisted and smug. The midafternoon sunlight elevated to an ominous glare.

Within minutes, two businessmen in a van stopped to help push the car farther off the road and agreed to take David to a phone in the next town. Sean settled into a grassy spot with a good book and I paced (that's what I do) from shock and worry, watching the traffic for possible assistance from the police. Adding insult, each truck driver simply had to hoot and holler, but I soon developed a technique of obvious snubbing (even if only I perceived it). I began a long litany of curses at the American car rental company we had chosen. The rustic beauty around me seemed incongruous to our mission there; whenever I lost myself in the vista, adrenaline reminded me that we were veritable sitting ducks, tourist variety.

Such a long time passed before a police scooter arrived that I imagined David might have already alerted the authorities and the rental office. The officer got out and swaggered my way, eyeing first the car, then me, then Sean, then me again. He stopped (closer than an American cop, but that was a cultural orientation, I knew), gallantly bowed, and tipped his cap.

"*Buenos tardes, señora.*"

Well, *señora* was still a bit of a shock, but not as much as the realization that I'd have to converse with him in Spanish. The thrill of the challenge surged with gut-wrenching apprehension. Oh well, at least I could say *buenos días*—oops, *tardes*—and perhaps fall back on my Italian soul for help. Might as well plunge in.

"*El niño . . .*" Would he think I meant my bookworm son? But no, of course, he'd know that I knew to say *hijo. . . .* "*El niño camine al camino . . .*" Could that be right? What next? Oh, there, that incredible hulk. I fairly danced over to the metal as I mimed driving over it and pointed wildly at the car's hidden gouged gas tank. He nodded pensively; I had no idea if anything was getting across. Nor could I stop myself.

"*Mi esposo . . . ,*" I went on. Now, where did that word . . . but, of course, the Italian was serving me; even if he wasn't really my husband, it seemed a better choice than *compañero* just then. I went on to mime and maim various words that could possibly make up hitchhiking and telephoning in the next town: "*San Juan del Río, no?*" "*Uno kilómetro, no?*" Then I masterfully displayed my concern over time. Would he *por favor* go find *mi esposo*?

A wild series of questions, gesticulations, and rounds of bilingual charades later, I understood that what he really wanted was to get me into the gas-dripping car to steer as he pushed it further off the road. No way. No way in hell was I getting in there. It was fine where it was. Go look for *mi esposo*, I politely stumbled through, give him a ride back, and then we can really do something about this mess. His parting bow seemed agreeable, leaving me flush with hope.

As he disappeared, a fit of laughter overtook me at the scene replaying in my head; I pried Sean loose from his book to listen to me tell what he had already overheard. But I needn't have laughed so hard; it was merely a rehearsal for the highway workers and cops who followed. Soon I grew tired of my usual lines and improvised madly, shocking myself with vocabulary scraped from the caverns of my mind. When the first cop returned, he'd think I'd used the time for a crash course at Berlitz. For all my horror at the situation, I was giddy with linguistic independence, imagining the parameters of this fish story when I finally got to tell David.

David . . . more than an hour and no sign. The cop returned and shrugged at my "what?-no-*esposo*" speech. Trying futilely to get me behind the wheel again, he left the instant I refused. My injured pride was joined by indignation at his indifference to my rational, and eloquent requests.

Six o'clock—an hour and a half since David had taken off with complete strangers. I thought the town was just down the road. The prickly splendor of the *nopales* grew rich with shadow as I recalled how we sometimes visualized parking spaces in our Brooklyn neighborhood, and mused about getting it to work. I was, after all, in the midst of a culture as steeped in the metaphysical as the culture of my ancestors. It was worth a try.

Whatever the reason, David arrived in a local taxi five minutes later, swearing at the enormous fare and lack of cooperation from the car rental office. They would come, with luck, by eight or nine. Suddenly starving, we divvied up the last of the crackers and oranges. As night approached, we moved the car off the shoulder, far from the drying gas. We sat inside with the doors open, taking in the gloaming time and the cricket song in lapses of traffic. David took a photo of the metal hunk, saying it would be important for insurance issues, but we knew it would end up in the family album.

At nine o'clock, with Sean still reading by flashlight and my tale of linguistic successes elaborated to death, David began to snore and I took a few winks here and there. Every check of the watch increased my anger, helplessness, and discomfort. My batteries were charging.

At 11:30, a car ground to a halt on the gravel ahead, shocking us out of our wits: Of the three men who converged on the car, only the third finally sported company identification. I gasped as one threw a lighted cigarette, luckily toward the road. We jumped out, Sean and I in the thick of it with David, the Spanish flying around my head like the Italian of my childhood. They inspected, two underneath, the third circling around with the three of us in procession behind him. David interpreted only that, along with the gas tank, the brake line had been sliced. He was casting uncertain looks at their work vehicle, clearly not one to relish for our vacation. Then our brief exchange of words was overtaken by something bigger and utterly mysterious.

"What's going on?" I badgered, that old child-as-outsider surfacing. David could hardly pause in what had certainly become a fight. But that was my role, and I couldn't even figure out a word, much less get one in! David could see me champing to get into the ring and I could see he preferred I stay out of it. He knew the take-charge business side of me that wouldn't quit, much less wilt from shyness over language. But this was his culture, one he knew and could negotiate.

Then either I got louder or they got quieter or there was simply a pause for breath. David turned to me. "They want more money—another open credit card voucher. And they want us to wait while they fix it. That's not what they said on phone." Vocabulary still hanging in the air now made sense to me. I'd known more than I had trusted myself to know.

The on-site manager was fumbling incongruously with a credit card imprinter, but soon the talk started up again, and I don't know how it happened but my comprehension soared. The two mechanics crawled out from under to join in. It could have been a bunch of Italian men on Bleecker Street in Utica where I grew up. Sure, I knew there was a cultural framework in operation, but I just couldn't help myself. Plus, I seethed at the perception that I was utterly invisible.

When the showdown arrived—open voucher or no work—I knew it by the stance. Without another thought, I jumped in front of David, shouting self-righteously, *"Pourquoi?"* Complete silence. No answer to a perfectly reasonable question? I mentally slapped my forehead: *Pourquoi?* Oh no, that's French, how could I? In seconds, the men simply started up again without me, my words mere static.

Now I was not to be deterred. I went a new round with a few tried and true applicable Spanish words. My approach was pure reason, one I'd learned at my father's knees. When that failed, I asserted my emphatic multilingual "no" to back up David's. To no avail. Transparency still plagued me. Then, as the yelling escalated, I found myself jumping in, with wringing hands this time, imploring, *"Por favor. Por favor. Mi hijo. La noche. ¡Por favor!"*

Immediate silence, attention. I could be seen. They stared at me, turned to each other, and shrugged. When they talked, it was, of course, directed to David, but the tone shifted to negotiation. Within minutes, we were being driven in the dirty, smelly service car to the next city, Querétaro, where we could argue the rest long distance to the main office. At 2:00 A.M., after winning at least cancellation of the remaining contract, we found a hotel. David swore a few blue streaks, as satisfying to me as my mother's Italian curses ever were.

It wasn't that I preferred that Carolina stay out; I innately knew that to the men I was confronting, it was beyond mere culture at the level we were dealing. If I had to refocus my linguistic neurons at the peak exchange, I would risk losing a cue, a clue, or an opportunity to maintain that I was not some gringo tourist who had encountered a misfortune they saw as potential for monetary gain. I had learned these strategies and tactics as a child, when I would occasionally take American tourists on nontraditional tours of the city's historical and cultural attractions.

Even with my cultural tactical arsenal, the situation demanded strict attention. I knew from numerous meetings and conferences where I have served as simultaneous translator that it is a huge and exhausting mental effort that requires intense focus. Carolina was never out of my sight, either visually or a third-eye sense of where she stood—both physically and on the multiple issues at hand. I had to wait until these men could hear as well as see her before her input about our plight could be a meaningful contribution. Prior to that, she would just be another adversary—and an annoying one at that because she was talking in foreign languages associated with the most poignant and painful history of military imperialist aggressions against México.

The moment she took on the role of a mother protecting her child, though, she touched the same chord that's at the root of el día de las madres. As a rule, we take mothers so seriously in México that Mother's Day isn't a mere second Sunday in May but is a national festive holiday—10 de mayo—on whatever day it falls. That is to say, we revere and we obey our mothers, even though we may stray on our own paths as adults.

On the bus to Guanajuato the next day, I recovered my good feelings about México and its warm friendly people who were everywhere but in the dreadful clutches of that American-Mexican car rental firm. The night before, I puzzled over what had happened in those last few moments of confrontation; the shift in my standpoint had not been deliberate or conscious. Reflecting with David and Sean, the picture began to emerge. On some level, I had made a decision to abandon my fierce woman warrior identity and revert to a cultural icon. An assertive American female could achieve nothing there. But do what a woman is "supposed to do"—appeal to men for help—and you become a sister or a mother or at least a *señora* in need. It didn't matter that a man was arguing the same case. The supplication of a mother for herself and her child could not be ignored. That I knew in my gut. I never had to learn that cultural code; I grew up in it.

Whatever my interference did or did not accomplish, however much as I disliked adopting that traditional female role, I understood the poetry of such a move. I had engaged in a kind of "mushfake discourse," what linguist James Paul Gee (1996) constructs from the prison culture term for making do with "something less when the real thing is not available" (p. 147). Through mushfake, I had linked my spotty language skills with "meta-knowledge" and created strategies to make do in an untenable situation. I had spoken the culture—and fluently. I enrolled in classes for the language again as soon as I got home.

Reference

Gee, J. (1996). *Social linguistics and literacies: Ideology in discourses* (2nd ed.). Bristol, PA: Falmer.

24

Listening for the Tao in Eight Tones

LINDA PETRUCELLI

Conventional wisdom tells us that the first step in language acquisition is not to speak but to listen. For nearly nine years I practiced the fine art of listening while I served as a missionary on the island of Taiwan. The lessons I learned from studying the Southern Min dialect however, were not exclusively linguistic. Perhaps more important, the experience of learning Taiwanese expanded my spiritual vocabulary.

In fact, my very first lesson occurred before I had even enrolled in language school. My husband and I had just moved into an apartment in Kaohsiung, Taiwan's "Scenic City of Heavy Industry" and one of Asia's largest ports. We hadn't even unpacked yet when our next door neighbors came calling and invited us over on a Sunday outing.

Mr. and Mrs. Liang were typical of Taiwan's new middle class: One car, two children, two jobs, and a shiny apartment far away from their rural roots. Their invitation was part hospitality and part curiosity, fueled by a strong desire to practice their English.

Most thirtysomething Taiwanese have grown up spending countless hours in school memorizing obscure grammatical rules in an effort to learn English, the language of international business and success. While the Liangs could easily read complex English sentences, their verbal skills were much less developed. As we rode in their car, our polite conversation was punctuated by long silences and questions about how to pronounce certain words.

As Mrs. Liang and I sat in the back seat, she suddenly turned to me and in her most practiced English asked, "Now why do you believe in two gods?"

"Two gods?" I repeated back to her. Surely she was confused.

"Yes, two gods," she insisted. "Why do you Christians believe in two gods?" I could understand one god or maybe even three, but two gods? I was dumbfounded.

"Of course you believe in two gods," she reasoned with me, "Why else would you have a Catholic god named *Thian-chu* (Lord of Heaven) and a Protestant god named *Siong-te* (Emperor Above All)?

There was no doubt that she had me. As an ordained minister in a justice-centered Protestant church, I went to Taiwan with the historical understanding of how often 19th-century colonialism and the mission movement coincided. But I was simply not prepared to confront the practical implications of exporting European Reformation history. In an effort to promulgate the oneness of God, my mission forebears had translated quite another message for Mrs. Liang.

The Highs and Lows of Imperfect Pitch

Walk any street in Taiwan and be prepared for a fascinating multifaith experience. The island's religious ethos is a heady mixture of Buddhism, Taoism, and ancestor worship oriented around a lunar calendar. Christianity accounts for only about 5% of its 21 million population. I was sent to work in partnership with the Presbyterian Church in Taiwan (PCT), the oldest and largest Protestant denomination on the island. An indigenous and self-supporting religious body, the PCT is internationally known as a champion of human rights and political self-determination for the Taiwanese people.

The majority of PCT members identify themselves as native Taiwanese whose ancestors immigrated from China's Fujian province over 400 years ago and whose mother tongue is Southern Min. This is in distinct contrast to the more recent arrivals of Mainlander Chinese, who fled to Taiwan with Chiang Kai-shek after the Communist revolution. Even though the Mainlanders make up less than 15% of the population, they ruled the island as a one-party state for 40 years until martial law was lifted in 1987.

The Mainlander ruling party, whose lingua franca is Mandarin, discouraged the use of Taiwanese and in certain settings outlawed it. Many of my Taiwanese friends recall how they were fined and even slapped for speaking their mother tongue in elementary school. In innumerable subtle and not so subtle ways, it was communicated that speakers of Taiwanese were less cultured, less educated, and less important. Whenever Taiwanese speakers made an appearance on television or radio, they were inevitably portrayed as buffoons or hicks.

When the PCT Language Committee determined that I would learn Taiwanese instead of Mandarin, I was not deterred by the political or cultural identity I knew I would necessarily assume. My fears were much more mundane. It was those eight changing tones that gave me the shivers.

Like many Asian tongues, Taiwanese is a tonal language that carries the meaning of words through vocal pitch. Most foreigners in Taiwan choose to learn Mandarin because of its relatively simple syntax and stable four-tone structure. Expats also learn Mandarin because it is the "official" language of schools, the courts, and the government and is therefore politically correct. Students of Taiwanese, however, are assaulted by a manic opera in eight tones that change according to a grammatical system with as many exceptions as rules. While my Mandarin schoolmates were spontaneously ordering noodles and buying train tickets after four weeks of class, I was still struggling with how to get out of the pronunciation guide.

Despite my previous language study, which included French, Nepali, Biblical Greek, and Hebrew, I was regularly stymied by Taiwanese. I took one-on-one tutorial instruction for three hours a day, five grueling days a week. While I quickly mastered the system of romanization (roman letters representing sounds and accent marks representing tones, which function as written Taiwanese in lieu of Chinese characters), I flunked my first oral exam after studying for days. In hindsight, my problem was grammatical inflexibility. To learn Taiwanese, I needed—to use a Taoist metaphor—to bend like bamboo in the wind.

For example, since my earliest college classes it was drilled into me never to use double negatives. But in Taiwanese, double negatives are considered to be an artful grammatical construction. "You *couldn't possibly not want to eat that . . . know him . . . go there.*" I was taught that directness in language was something to be desired. But in Taiwanese there is no simple *yes* or *no.* I also learned the unwritten rule that passive speech should be avoided at all cost. However, Taiwanese sentence construction regularly relies on the passive.

Even my notions of time became less rigid and less linear. There are no tenses per se in Taiwanese. Verbs are not declined but are used to denote degrees of completed or incompleted action. Time words (*yesterday, now, later*) are used if more precision is required. As I let the winds of Taiwanese grammar and syntax whisk me in new directions, I began to notice a curious deterioration in my ability to pen a cogent letter home.

Nothing about Taiwanese, however, challenged me more than learning how to sing eight tones. The same syllable can mean radically different things or connote no meaning at all if spoken with a different tone. Tonal changes occur depending on what precedes a syllable and where a word is placed in a sentence and custom—my Taiwanese teachers would tell me with a smile, "We say it because it makes better music."

My major difficulty was the way I processed emotion through vocal variety. I am second-generation Italian-American and am accustomed to STRESS-ing certain words to add COL-or and EMPH-asis. Unfortunately, this habit of mine unintentionally altered tones and consequently changed what I said.

It was eight months of nonstop language study and diligent practice in open-air markets, noodle stands, and tea shops before I summoned enough nerve to deliver my first Taiwanese sermon. As I meticulously prepared and practiced singing my tones, I inwardly prayed for a sign that I was in the right place, speaking the right language, at the right time.

Standing before the congregation of Chian-Kim Church, I could see there wasn't an empty pew in the sanctuary. I cleared my throat, took a sip of water, fought my terror, and began to speak. Though I can barely recall the subject of my homily, I will never forget uttering one sentence in particular.

It had been my intention to say, "Jesus went about teaching all the people" (*Ia-so' ka-si lang*). Not an inappropriate message to hear in church on Sunday morning. But I didn't realize that my pitch went one way when it should have gone another (*Ia-so ka-si lang~*). And that one deceptively simple tone lead me to proclaim with firm conviction that "Jesus went about biting all the people to death!"

I couldn't help but wonder what God was trying to tell me.

My Third Ear Opens

When the pastor of Chian-Kim Church and a valued mentor, Ong Bok-su, discretely informed me of my faux pas in the pulpit, I realized that I must have been unconsciously making such embarrassing language blunders all the time. Learning Taiwanese would have been a much more daunting task, however, if it hadn't been for the good-natured forgiveness of the Taiwanese people. In fact, my pronouncement of Jesus's eating habits was not the only mistake I had made during my sermon.

Ong Bok-su gently explained that the language of the church often relies on entirely different vocabulary than that of secular speech. When I offered thanks to God during a prayer, I unwittingly used the secular words for *thank you*. Likewise, Biblical and theological language is not commonly used during everyday speech—not even in Christian households.

So my meager linguistic background did not provide even the religious basics necessary for a worship service. Worse yet, however, was my misunderstanding of the two Taiwanese forms of "we." I consistently used "Goan" instead of "Lan." The former suggests a certain exclusivity because the "we" does not include the person being addressed. "Lan," on the other hand, is an inclusive we, connoting me and whoever is hearing me, and suggests the kind of connected relationship and intimacy good preaching requires.

How would I ever find a message worth sharing? I wondered. And would I ever develop enough skill to articulate it so as to be understood? The revelation of my own inadequacies, even after enormous effort, left me disquieted.

"I know you are really *thia* by Taiwanese," I thought I heard Ong Bok-su say to me. I was "pained" by Taiwanese. You could say that again. He said this with such warm and affirming conviction, however, that I assumed I had misunderstood him.

When Ong Bok-su repeated once again that seemingly simple sentence, I paid closer attention. I listened with my third ear and then carried his words home with me, where I immediately sat down in the study and searched for *thia* in my romanized dictionary.

Thia, I learned, is a homonym meaning pain but also love. The love it describes is not the secular but is more akin to the deep love that God has for the world, and is reserved to describe the most meaningful of human relationships and endeavors.

Ong Bok-su was telling me that I really "loved" Taiwanese. What began as one of the most discouraging moments in my checkered career as a language student ended in epiphany. From that moment forward, I began hearing the language of Taiwanese in a new way, receiving from its irregular quirks and syntaxical detours a plethora of everyday wisdom and meaning.

The Word Finds the Path

A year later I left classroom studies and began my full-time work. It was then that my communication skills began to develop at an accelerated pace. I was assigned to a church-sponsored social service center that offered outreach training programs to the island's fishing community. The Fishermen's Service Center (FSC) was staffed with a former fish worker as director, three local workers, and myself. All of us shared responsibility for casework, community education, and organizing.

Each afternoon, my Taiwanese colleagues and I would go visiting in homes, where I learned through silent observation the unspoken vocabulary of body language and gesture—how to comfort a mother whose son is lost at sea. How to say thanks for a steaming bowl of eel (and actually appear to mean it). How to tell the difference between a purse seiner, a pair trawler, and a hook-and-line vessel.

Very few of the families we assisted in Kaohsiung were Christian. Most of them had been engaged in offshore fishing for generations and practiced general veneration of *Mat-so*, a protective female guardian of seafarers and fishermen. At times I found myself anxiously wondering how these mostly poor and semiliterate fishers would relate to our Christian organization.

Initially, I feared that we would be viewed as do-gooding outsiders at best, perhaps even as arrogant fanatics at worst. Thankfully, neither of these extremes prevailed, as solidarity and service to those in need erased most of our economic, class, and religious differences.

The FSC wisely operated on the principle of no strings attached. Our staff arranged women's support groups, organized fishermen to advocate for more protective legislation, helped negotiate insurance claims, and offered a whole variety of other services entirely without cost or expectation that those we assisted should convert to Christianity.

The one explicitly religious witness of the FSC was a form of interfaith prayer that regularly occurred before travel (a good idea, given Taiwan's traffic), preceding meals, and with any fishing family who had experienced the injury or death of a loved one. This approach won much respect and admiration in non-Christian circles.

Unfortunately, not all believers understood the wisdom of this. I still recall the British minister who was appalled that the FSC gratefully received offerings of money from the local Buddhists. The British pastor believed that since the money had come from people who believed in idols, it should be rejected on principle. How wonderful it was to work with Taiwanese Christians who believed no such thing.

In fact, the FSC often presented its educational seminars for fishermen in the outdoor courtyard of our office's neighborhood temple. On one such occasion a female monk approached me and asked if I understood the Tao. I sheepishly admitted that I only knew it was a word that meant the Path.

"If you listen for it," she said, "you will hear much more. The Tao," she told me, "is where your God and my God meet."

Deconstructing Definitions

As my language skills expanded, so did my responsibilities at work. I was regularly invited to give the *Ko'-le* (encouraging words) at fisher gatherings. At such moments I often told traditional proverbs like, "For every leaf there is at least one drop of dew," and "Those who get on the boat first, get off the boat last." I continued to reflect upon pain and love as well as another homonym, *hi-bang*, which means both *fishnet* and *hope*.

The work of the FSC also expanded as we became increasingly involved with labor concerns in the distant-water deep-sea fishing sector and its crew, primarily non-Chinese tribals, sometimes known as the Mountain People of Taiwan. Nobody really knows for certain when the Mountain People arrived on the island, but estimates trace their ancestors back at least 1,000 years.

Preferring to call themselves "the Original People," these 10 tribes of Malayo-Polynesian stock now number only around 350,000 and suffer from many social problems such as alcoholism, unemployment, and severe discrimination. Because of their strong physiques and relative innocence, their young people are persistently wooed onto Taiwan's high-tech oceangoing fishing vessels for extremely low wages.

On one of our staff trips to the less developed east coast, where many of the Original People live, I was asked to present an educational segment warning the village about the dangers of underground fishing agents and their unscrupulous methods of luring naïve teenage boys onto the boats without their parents' permission. Mayau, a young man from the Ami tribe, was assigned to translate my Taiwanese into the villagers' mother tongue.

"When strangers enter your village," I began and then waited for Mayau's translation. He cocked his head, paused longer than I thought necessary, and asked me to repeat myself.

"When you see strangers enter your village," I began again. But Mayau still look confused. "I can't translate that," he said to me. So I repeated myself yet another time, only much louder. "When there are strangers in your village," I shouted. "Don't you understand the word *stranger?*"

Mayau shook his head. "I can't translate that, " he said. "In our language," Mayau explained with an authority that pulled and pinched my third ear, "there is no word for *stranger—only honored and welcomed guest*."

There is a Taoist saying that water, the softest of substances, makes smooth the roughest rocks. Certainly the experience of learning to speak Taiwanese wore smooth even the roughest sides of my personality. The long process of learning Taiwanese allowed me to attend—with my third ear—to a new rhetoric of the spirit. For it was through my eight-toned journey that I came to understand the Tao, not only as a path to walk along, but also as a bar of music to sing, a bridge to cross cultures, and an encounter to link faiths . . . one fragile reed of bamboo gently dipping with the wind.

25

Learning Language/Learning Self

KAREN OGULNICK

One of my first childhood friends in Flushing, New York, was a Chinese girl named Wendy who lived next door. Except for my grandparents' house, where Yiddish was spoken frequently, Wendy's house was the only place where I recall hearing a language other than English. I experimented with my own version of "Chinese" at home, stringing together the Chinese sounds I heard at Wendy's house. My grandfather heard me and became intrigued. "Can you really speak Chinese?" he asked me. When I insisted that I was really speaking Chinese, he proceeded to quiz me, just to be sure: "How do you say this in Chinese?" he'd ask as he pointed to various household objects, and I'd promptly come up with my own Chinese version. "Mary, she's speaking Chinese!" My grandmother nodded her head and smiled in a way that said she wasn't convinced. But Grandpa's enthusiasm remained strong, and became an even greater source of amusement to the rest of the family than my newly discovered linguistic talent. Every once in a while someone in my family recalls the time "when Grandpa really believed [I] could speak Chinese."

Ever since I was very young, I wanted to travel. When I was 19 I finally had my first chance to travel abroad. As a college student in London, I lived in an international hostel with other foreign students, most of whom were from Asia and Africa. We would take turns cooking and tasting one another's cultures—Indonesian, Indian, Malaysian, Thai, Chinese, Iranian, Tunisian, Ethiopian. I also contributed a dish of my own: spaghetti à la Bronx. After four months of our dinners together not only did I develop a taste for hotter and spicier foods, but the many stories I heard about the faraway places and the people my friends were so homesick for gave me a craving to travel more extensively. A few months later, I did. What began as an invitation to spend the Chinese New Year with friends in Hong Kong turned into a 13-month journey through Southeast Asia.

As I traveled from one country to another, I enjoyed communicating primarily through gestures. I imagined that I could read minds and send telepathic messages. I focused on facial expressions and zoomed in on eye contact. There were many times when I wanted to know what people were actually saying; however, I also often sensed that I was at a distinct advantage not knowing. Ambiguity felt liberating. I didn't have to conform as much to expectations or behavior that I might consider restrictive. I could move in and out of culturally imposed definitions more freely.

While being a traveler gave me an enormous sense of freedom, living in a foreign country for an extended period of time was a different experience altogether. I first went to Japan in 1985 to teach English in Japanese high schools. Before my departure, I spoke not even one word of Japanese. (Well, maybe "sushi"). I convinced myself that people in Japan could speak English, and if they couldn't, I was planning on teaching it to them. Almost immediately upon my arrival on that cold, wet July day, I realized, when nobody spoke English, that learning Japanese might be a good idea. In spite of what I understood logically, I made very little if any effort to do so. On one level, I wanted to be included in the culture, but on another, I felt comfortable remaining outside it. I also was convinced that it would be almost impossible for me to learn Japanese. Aside from my stint at Chinese, I did not consider myself a good language learner.

To my surprise, my extremely limited Japanese did not prevent me from making friends with people who didn't speak English. I even learned, to some degree, *sado* (tea ceremony) and *ikebana* (flower arrangement). These classes were recommended to me by my supervising teacher at the high school because they were considered appropriate for young single women. They were conducted entirely in Japanese. I also watched a lot of TV. Without understanding a word, I was thoroughly engrossed in the soap operas, samurai dramas, sumo wrestling matches, *animé* (cartoons), even the commercials.

I worked six long days a week in Japanese schools. On the seventh day I was usually invited to attend an outing with Japanese colleagues or friends. I spent months not understanding most of what people said. (This was often the case even when they spoke English.) At this point I was becoming more confident in my interpretations of body language, pitch, tone, volume, and silence. I felt I could sense the emotional climate—when an interaction was harmonious and when I thought someone was being overly polite, stiff, and compliant. It was reassuring to think that I had at least *some* idea of what was going on.

The first time I realized I was absorbing Japanese occurred about three months after I first arrived in Japan. One day while I was riding on a streetcar on my way to work, an elderly woman entered at one of the stops and sat down right next to me in the empty car. When she began to speak to me in Japanese I cut her off with an expression I memorized— *zenzen wakarimasen*—I can't understand a word of what you're saying. This didn't seem to discourage her, however, from continuing to talk to me. I just smiled and nodded as she spoke and felt relieved when we arrived at her stop, at which point I waved her off with the one other word (in addition to *sushi*) that comprised my entire active Japanese vocabulary—*sayonara*. Once alone with my thoughts, I realized that I had understood some of what she had said, something about the weather, and that the entire conversation was in Japanese. This sudden awareness—that I was beginning to learn Japanese—was exhilarating. From that moment on, I could no longer resist being swept up in the current of Japanese language and culture.

The first stage of my verbal ability consisted of imitating what I heard. This posed several problems, since it is not always appropriate for two speakers to use the same level of politeness and formality with one another. For instance, when speaking with my landlord, an elderly grandmother, I repeated words and expressions that are typically spoken to children. Similarly, I responded to shopkeepers and other people providing services with the same extremely polite expressions with which they greeted me, such as *irrashaimase* (welcome), which prompted some startled looks from people who apparently were not used to customers greeting them back in honorific language. I also picked up some "male" and regional expressions from friends and colleagues, which may have sounded cute and funny in some contexts, such as when we were out drinking, but in more serious situations, these same expressions became crude and disrespectful. I could tell by the grimaces on people's faces. People rarely corrected me directly; on the contrary, they showered me with praise: "*Nihongo ga o-jouzu desu ne*" (your Japanese is very good), to which I often responded by saying, "Thank you." Another no-no. It took me a while, but finally I realized that the compliments were intended as an indirect way of correcting me.

One of these occasions was when I met a high school principal for the first time. Before leaving his office I bowed and said *gokuroosamadeshita* (thank you very much). He responded by telling me how well I spoke Japanese, which prompted me to thank him again. He bowed and responded with a different thank you, *osukaresamadeshita*. Outside his office, a Japanese English teacher was kind enough to enlighten me on the many different "thank you"s in Japanese, depending on whom you are thanking for what. Apparently, I thanked the principal for doing some demeaning work for me. That's when he told me how well I spoke Japanese. The second time he thanked me for my trouble (realizing I was having a hard time learning the language). It would have been more appropriate to use a polite expression that is used in a formal context: *domo arigato gozaimasu*. It didn't take long for me to learn the ubiquitous *sumimasen* (*thank you* that also means *excuse me*), and the more humble and polite *osoreirimasu* (*thank you* that also means *I'm sorry*). With friends I learned to be more casual with *arigato*, or even more intimately, *domo* (thanks). And (this one took me a while) I learned that when someone compliments you, it is more appropriate to modestly reject it, *iie, sono koto wa arimasen* (oh no, not at all), than to say "thank you."

Even in the use of directions, the Japanese have still found a way to express their status and humility. As a world traveler, I had developed some confidence in my sense of direction. This was shaken when I began to travel independently in Japan. I've always taken for granted that "up" means north and "down" means south, but that is not always the case in Japan, which made train travel confusing, since trains are referred to as "up" or "down" trains. Since all trains arriving at Tokyo are called "up" trains, the important thing to know, apparently, is not the actual direction you are going, but whether the city of your destination has a higher or lower socio-economic status than the one you started from.

Status is also marked in the psychological and geographical division of Japan into two parts: western Japan (the side facing China), also known as "the backside," and eastern Japan, "the frontside." The contradiction one faces is that with all the lip service given to "tradition" in Japanese culture, it is the more modern and future-oriented "frontside" of Japan that is afforded higher status, as people who reside in Japan's "backside," self-effacingly refer to themselves as "country bumpkins."

Because my job required a lot of traveling, I had many opportunities to meet people. If I had my own car, I probably wouldn't have learned as much Japanese. The trains and buses were the best language laboratories. While in transit, it might have looked as though I was reading an English newspaper, but more often I'd be eavesdropping on the conversation behind me, sometimes even taking notes. I also had to ask for directions often and found it very encouraging when people not only understood me, but responded and sometimes initiated further conversation in Japanese. There were even a few surprising occasions when I became involved in deep discussions.

Similar to the way people sometimes tell fellow travelers their life stories, women I barely knew shared intimate details of their lives with me. While being invited in this way into people's lives helped to make me feel more inside the culture, telling me their stories may have been a way for Japanese women to connect with the outside world. I was told tales of forced arranged marriages that made me feel relieved to be American. I believed I was freer than these Japanese women I had met. In contrast to the supermodern image that the American press promoted of Japan prior to my initial departure in 1984, the society in which I was living reminded me more of an ancient time when women were controlled and constrained to activities and roles revolving around the household.

When I returned to Japan for the third time in 1993, I saw things quite differently. This time, looking at Japanese women seemed more like looking into a mirror, not one that reflected back my exact image, but one that revealed, even where there were differences, much about the condition of being a woman in my own culture. As a thirty-two year-old single Jewish American woman living in Hiroshima, I contemplated the contradictions of learning to speak and of being silenced by a culture. My inside/outside location as a participant-observer in Japan gave me a vantage point from where I could notice oppressive structures in both Japan and the United States, particularly how they pertain to women, which is difficult to do from a space within the culture. The glass ceiling became more visible.

Ironically, learning the importance that role status plays in communication—that levels of politeness and formality are governed by such factors as age, class, social position, and gender—inhibited me: I felt self-conscious and afraid of making mistakes that would make me look like a stupid, unrefined American in many Japanese people's eyes. My desire to fit in as much as possible to the society that was nurturing my new Japanese persona motivated me to work on producing softer, more polite and refined ways of speaking. The way Japanese was affecting me physically did not occur to me until the first time I saw myself on a video, which a friend taped at the end of my second year in Japan. I watched this non-Japanese woman, sitting demurely on her knees, delicately covering her mouth with her hands as she giggled, speaking in a high-pitched tone of voice. She seemed so Japanese. I knew that she had my face and hair, but I could hardly recognize the rest of myself.

Through learning Japanese I learned something about my first language and culture, which leads me to conclude that there is a dialectic between language learning and identity that is inextricably linked to our historical experiences and the sociopolitical contexts in which we find ourselves. Beyond knowing words and grammar, learning a language involves acquiring a role, and knowing how to act according to that social definition. It is knowing, sometimes tacitly, sometimes consciously, what others approve and disapprove of, how to sit, how to enter a room, how to read nuances, when to speak and when to be silent, how to accept a gift, how to ask for a favor, how to ward off unwanted invitations. Knowing this is also inhabiting, willingly and unwillingly, consciously and subconsciously, a location in the hierarchy. In other words, language learning entails a process of fitting into one's place in society, or rather, one's imposed place.

About the Contributors

Mimi Bluestone has worked as a journalist and editor for more than 20 years. She has served as editor of *Sing Out!*, a folk music magazine; science editor at *Business Week;* director of publications for INFORM, an environmental research organization; and a freelance writer for a variety of magazines. She is writing a biography for young adults of Rose Pesotta, a union organizer who brought thousands of women into the labor movement in the 1930s. She currently teaches English in the New York City public schools.

Sharon Shelton Colangelo is a faculty member of the English Department at Northwest Vista College in San Antonio, Texas. She is the author of *Voices of Student Teachers: Cases from the Field* (Prentice Hall) and numerous journal articles. She was president of LEARN, an organization of English and language arts educators. She is in the centennial edition of *Who's Who in America*.

Susan Driscoll graduated from Teachers College, Columbia University, with her M.A. in Teaching English to Speakers of Other Languages in the spring of 1997 and taught English at Ewha Woman's University in Seoul, Korea.

Elizabeth Dykman received her Ph.D. in Multilingual/Multicultural Studies at New York University. She taught graduate courses in the TESOL (Teaching English to Speakers of Other Languages) Program. She was trained as an architectural designer, and spoke of five languages. Sadly, Elizabeth passed away on December 18, 2002.

Margie English lives in Vermont, where she works as an employment specialist and a case manager on a Deaf services team for health care and rehabilitation services in Brattleboro.

Stephanie Hart is a writer and teacher of writing and literature to English-language learners at the Fashion Institute of Technology and Parsons School of Design. She has written and published in a variety of genres, including young adult fiction, short stories, essays, and memoirs.

George Jochnowitz is a professor of linguistics at the College of Staten Island, City University of New York. He writes about a variety of subjects, including the language of the Jews of Italy and the political situation in contemporary China. His work has appeared in such places as *Weekly Standard*, *Dissent*, *Midstream*, *La Rassegna Mensile di Israel*, and *American Speech*.

Christina Kotchemidova holds a *licence en lettres* from the University of Lausanne, Switzerland, and an M.A. in journalism from New York University. She is currently a Ph.D. candidate in Mass Media at NYU. Her publications include articles and essays in the Bulgarian and American press, chapters in books of criticism, and introductions to volumes of Western literature published in Bulgarian. Kotchemidova has also translated works by Susan Sontag, Nadine Gordimer, Gore Vidal, James Agee, Truman Capote, Paul Valery, Albert Camus, and many others into Bulgarian.

Carolina Mancuso teaches in the Master of Science in Teaching program at New School University and holds an M.A. and a Ph.D. in English Education from New York University. She has had short stories, essays, and articles published in a variety of journals, magazines, and anthologies. One of her short stories won the Reed Smith Fiction Award and was nominated for the Pushcart Prize. She is pleased to report that she recently completed the intermediate level of Spanish.

Rita E. Negrón Maslanek is a human resources director for a national church organization in New York City. She holds a B.S. degree in business administration from Dominican College, Blauvelt, New York, and an A.A.S. degree in Accounting from New York City Community College. Ms. Maslanek currently resides in a suburb outside New York City with her husband of 28 years and two adult children.

Doug Millison is a writer and journalist based in El Cerrito, California. With designer and typographer David Siegel, he co-wrote and edited *Creating Killer Web Sites*, second edition, a bestselling book in 1997. He also writes fiction and is working on a novel.

Watson R. Millison was born in Santa Ana, California, in 1987. He attends East Bay French-American School (*École Bilingue*) in Berkeley, California. He is a prize-winning pianist (first place in the 1998 sonata competition of the Contra Costa County Music Teachers Association), competes on the

Albany Blue Dolphins Swim Team, and plays right field for the Pirates in the El Cerrito Youth Baseball League.

Raimundo Mora immigrated from Colombia to the United States in 1979. In 1982, he earned a master's degree in Teaching English to Speakers of Other Languages and in 1992, his doctorate in Bilingual Education. He has taught English as a Second Language and Bilingual Education for 18 years. Currently he is the Director of the ESL/Bilingual Program of Hudson County Community College, in New Jersey.

Greta Hofmann Nemiroff is co-director of the New School of Dawson College in Montréal, where she teaches English, Humanities, and Women's Studies. She is president of the Sisterhood is Global Institute, an international nongovernmental organization with projects in nine countries. She has written or edited seven books and published numerous articles and stories in books and journals.

Myrna Nieves is a writer, cultural activist, and educator from Puerto Rico. She is a professor at Boricua College, in Brooklyn, New York, where she coordinates a yearly Poetry Series. Her work has been published in several magazines, including *And Then, Brujula/Compass*, and *The Poetry Project*. In 1990 she co-published a bilingual book of poems and prose, *Tripartita: Earth, Dreams, Powers*, and in 1997 the University of Puerto Rico Press published her book of dreams, *Libreta De Sueños (Narraciones)*.

Elizabeth Nuñez is a professor of English language and literature at Medgar Evers College, the City University of New York. She received her Ph.D. and M.A. degrees in English from New York University, and her B.A. degree in English from Marian College in Wisconsin. Her publications include the novels *Bruised Hibiscus* and *Beyond the Limbo Silence*, which won the 1999 Independent Publishers Book Award in the multicultural fiction category; and *When Rocks Dance*. She is co-editor of the collection of essays *Defining Ourselves: Black Writers in the 90s*, and author of several monographs on literature and writing. Nunez is Director of the National Black Writers Conference, a project sponsored by the National Endowment for the Humanities.

Karen Ogulnick is director of the Programs of Teaching English to Speakers of Other Languages and Bilingual Education and associate professor of education at Long Island University, C. W. Post Campus. Her first book, *Onna Rashiku (Like a Woman): The Diary of a Language Learner in Japan*, was named Outstanding Work in Women's Studies by New York University's

Women's Studies Commission. She has also published various articles, essays, and short stories. A world traveler and lifelong language learner, she has presented her work on language and culture at conferences nationally and internationally.

Linda Petrucelli is an ordained minister with the United Church of Christ and holds advanced degrees from Yale Divinity School and Chicago Theological Seminary. Ms. Petrucelli currently serves as a national church executive, responsible for overseas programs of humanitarian relief, refugees, emergencies, and agricultural development.

David Rodgers was born and raised in México, D.F., and at 15 emigrated to United States. He received his B.A. in Latin American Studies from the University of Texas at El Paso and his M.A. in Foreign Languages and Literatures from Washington State University. Currently, he teaches and serves as college advisor at Newcomers High School, a public bilingual school in New York for new immigrants. In 1997, he participated in Project Sol, a National Endowment for the Humanities Institute, to develop interdisciplinary curricula, including Spanish, ESL, Art, and Social Studies, on the cultures of New Mexico. David is pursuing a Ph.D. at New York University.

Fredy Amilcar Roncalla was born in the Peruvian Andes in 1953. He grew up speaking Spanish and Quechua, the main indigenous language of Peru. He studied linguistics and literature at the Catholic University of Peru, and focused on anthropological field work in the Andes. He is the author of *Canto de pajaro o invocacion a la palabra*, a book of poetry, and *Escritos mitimaes: Hacia una poetica andina postmoderna*.

Robert Roth is a writer who lives in New York City. He co-edits the magazine *And Then*.

Ruby Sprott is a product of New York City. She currently teaches at the State University of New York College at Old Westbury, where she is an associate professor in the Teacher Education program and teaches multicultural education. She serves on the executive board of Riverside Church's Racial Justice and South Africa Initiatives. In 1995 she was invited to participate in the NGO (Non-Government Organization) Forum on Women in Beijing as a part of the International Association of University Presidents' delegation. She currently lives in Manhattan and has one son.

Verena Stefan is a Swiss-German writer of fiction and nonfiction, translator, and poet. Born in Bern, Switzerland, in 1947, she lived in Berlin from 1968 to 1975 and has immigrated to Canada. She is co-founder of the feminist group *Brot und Rosen* (Bread and Roses), with whom she published the *Frauenhandbuch Nr. 1*, on abortion and contraception, in 1972. She teaches women's studies and creative writing. Her books include *Haeutungen* (Frauenoffensive, 1975) translated as *Shedding* (Daughters, 1978); *Shedding, Literally Dreaming, Euphoria, and Cacophony* (Feminist Press, 1994), a collection of short stories; *Wortgetreu ich traeume* (Arche, 1987), translated as *Literally Dreaming* (Feminist Press, 1994); and *Es reich gewesen* (*Times Have Been Good*) (Fischer, 1993). She was a co- translator of Adrienne Rich's *The Dream of a Common Language* and of Monique Wittig and Sande Zeig's *Lesbian Peoples: Material for a Dictionary*. Her most recent book is a study of the figure of the girl in literature, *Rauh, wild & frei* (*Rough, Wild & Free*) (Fischer, 1997).

Susan Stocker is integrating her philosophical training with insights from feminism, literature, and emancipatory theater work to overcome the disassociation that love of theory induces. For this reason, she is also interested in first-person accounts of learning, the so-called "understory of achievement." She is an assistant professor in the Philosophy and Religion Department of Goucher College in Baltimore, Maryland.

Cora Acebrón Tolosa is a writer and scholar. She has master's degrees in English from the Universidad Complutense de Madrid and in Classics from Columbia University, where she is completing her doctorate. She has lived and taught in Spain, Italy, and the United States. She writes fiction and scholarship on Spanish literature, Latin literature, and gender studies. She teaches Latin at Shenandoah University, and lives in the countryside at the foot of the Blue Ridge Mountains in Virginia.

Pramila Venkateswaran teaches English and Women's Studies at Nassau Community College in New York. Her articles on global women's issues have appeared in *Women's Studies Quarterly*, and her poems on feminist themes have appeared in *Long Island Quarterly*, *Ariel: Journal of International English Literature*, and *Nassau*, among others.

Index